Housework and Gender
in American Television

Housework and Gender in American Television

Coming Clean

Kristi Rowan Humphreys

LEXINGTON BOOKS
Lanham • Boulder • New York • London

Published by Lexington Books
An imprint of The Rowman & Littlefield Publishing Group, Inc.
4501 Forbes Boulevard, Suite 200, Lanham, Maryland 20706
www.rowman.com

Unit A, Whitacre Mews, 26-34 Stannary Street, London SE11 4AB

British Library Cataloguing in Publication Information Available

Library of Congress Cataloging-in-Publication Data
Humphreys, Kristi Rowan, 1977– author.
Housework and gender in American television : coming clean / Kristi Rowan Humphreys.
    pages cm
Includes bibliographical references and index.
ISBN 978-0-7391-9252-8 (cloth : alk. paper) — ISBN 978-0-7391-9253-5 (electronic)
ISBN 978-1-4985-2988-4 (pbk : alk. paper)
1. Families on television. 2. Women on television. 3. Housewives—United States.
4. Housekeeping—United States. 5. Television programs—United States. I. Title.
PN1992.8.F33H86 2016
791.45'6552—dc23   2015033449

Printed in the United States of America

For my mother, Marilyn Rowan—my husband,
Chris—and my children, Rowan and Lawson

Contents

List of Figures

Acknowledgments

So many have helped in the creation of this book, but I will begin by thanking my editors Mimi Choi and Elizabeth Patton from my first housework chapter in *Home Sweat Home*. They saw something in my work and contributed much to the development of this larger project. I'd also like to thank Lindsey Porambo and Marilyn Ehm for their kindness and extraordinary guidance through the publication process. Edward Zimmerman and Sony Pictures Television have been incredibly generous in allowing me to use images from their holdings. I am indebted to Lydia Thompson, David Mondt, and Texas Tech University, who generously provided the funds and resources for this project. I have been so fortunate to have exceptional colleagues like Lydia and David all along the way.

I'm incredibly thankful to friends and colleagues Michael Markus and Ed Check, who gave numerous helpful suggestions. My graduate students at Texas Tech, especially fellow mothers Sarai Brinker and Renee Wilson, contributed greatly to my ideas and assessments. My colleague Heather Warren-Crow provided some of the best motivation and moral support I could ask for, especially during the final months, in addition to my sweet sister, Julie Evans, and father, Garland Rowan, who even watched the kids at times while I wrote.

Most important, I'd like to thank my mother, Marilyn Rowan, who is the kindest and most loving person I know. She makes me want to be a better mother every day, and I can only hope to give my own children a fraction of the care she has given me. This brings me to my husband, Chris, and sons, Rowan and Lawson. I am blessed beyond measure by a partner who wholeheartedly wants to share housework and parenting because he recognizes the lifelong rewards of such work, and I have no doubt our sons will be exceptional husbands and fathers because of the model he provides for them every single day. Thanks for supporting me boys, while I wrote my book.

Chapter 1

Introduction

During my first semester of graduate school, I was assigned to read Konstantin Stanislavsky's *My Life in Art* for a course on modern theater. I was excited and eager, until I discovered it to be a text of almost 600 pages. Committed to doing the work, I knew I would need a quiet space void of distractions to read, so I decided to drive to Houston, Texas, to spend a week at the tranquil home of my eighty-four-year-old grandmother, Juliana. She was elated I was visiting, saying, "Kristi, just finish your reading. I won't bother you at all." She tucked me away on a comfortable chair in a room off the kitchen. The first day, Grandma must have poked her head quietly into my room at least a dozen times, whispering, "I don't mean to bother you, but can I make you a sandwich? How about a glass of milk? I'm about to bake some cookies. Want some? Is it too warm in here? Want me to adjust the temperature?" To each question, I warmly replied, "no, thanks," hoping to devote as much time as possible to reading. Even as a rather selfish twenty-something, I noticed her disappointment in my answers, even if I did not understand it. After the first day, I started saying "yes" to all of her questions, whether I needed something or not: "Yes, Grandma, I would love a sandwich. A glass of milk sounds fantastic. Those cookies will surely hit the spot. I am a bit warm, actually." That week with her taught me so much about women, service, strength, feminism, and life. I regarded my grandmother as the strongest woman alive. She had lost her twin brother in her youth, lived through the depression and wars, lost her husband far too early in life, raised four children, and yet, she was the happiest, most fulfilled person I knew, eternally charging life in the raw. Grandma was always full of joy, but I never understood that joy until those seven days I spent with her during graduate school. Then, it hit me. She found joy in serving me, joy in serving others. This, in fact, was her strength.

When I began this project, I sought to write a book on housework, television, and women that would investigate, and perhaps clarify on a personal level, the discrepancies I was experiencing between reality and representation. Housework is an activity I have considered often throughout my life. Let me be clear; I have done quite a bit of *thinking* about housework. More specifically, I am messy and quite comfortable—perhaps too comfortable—living in a house that hasn't been dusted in months. I've been this way all my life, and even as a teenager, my mother, as many mothers do of their teenagers' rooms, often likened my room to a "tornado zone." Surprisingly, though, as I matured and began to maintain my own places, my tornado zone saw little change. Before motherhood, I simply never understood the fuss over housework.

I was lovingly reared by a CPA father and a nurse/homemaker mother on a ranch in a one-stoplight town in Texas, and my mom was largely responsible for the household management. She cooked and cleaned when she got home from work, as well as on the weekends. Some of my favorite childhood memories involve awakening on Saturday mornings, peeking out of my bedroom window, and finding mom in her tattered 1970s swimsuit (that she refuses to replace) mowing the lawn. Mom and I would often sit and watch television together, while she hovered over a laundry basket folding underwear and socks. I never offered to help her. I wish I had, but I viewed housework as "mom's job" and never questioned it. I didn't ask her how she felt about it, or if she wished someone would help her. I never even thanked her when my folded clothes magically appeared on the end of my bed. In those moments specifically, my thoughts were always more concentrated on the invasion of privacy that had occurred when she entered my bedroom. Ironically, when I became a wife and mother myself, I resisted any and all implications that housework was *my* job alone just because I was a woman.

As a child of the late 1970s and early 1980s, growing up on a ranch out in the country meant we had three television stations, and I will never forget the excitement my siblings and I experienced when we finally got the Fox channel. Much of the programming on our three and eventually four channels involved reruns from the 1950s and 1960s. Together, mom and I, more than any other member of our family, were drawn to these shows. I noticed early on distinct differences between the televised households and housewife characters and my own mother: they did much more housework and their homes were much cleaner. Sure, mom did all of the cooking and cleaning for a household of five, which means she did a lot, but where do you think I learned my poor dusting habits? Whether she meant to or not, through her actions, mom taught me that life is too short to worry constantly about dust, dirt, and clutter, and if this is the lesson she intended me to learn, she succeeded splendidly. More to the point, though, these television-viewing moments with my mother made me realize that I wanted to achieve a more comprehensive understanding of the relationships between housework, gender, love, preservation, and familial roles in our visual culture. (So, Mom, if any part of this introduction has embarrassed you, I hope you consider forgiving me when I credit you with inspiring this book. I understand if you want to finish the book before deciding.)

My first experience researching televised housework involved a chapter I wrote years ago titled "Supernatural Housework: Magic and Domesticity in 1960s Television" in the anthology *Home Sweat Home*. I had read various studies claiming "1950s sitcoms presented gender systems defined by domesticity, in which the mothers often assume background, devalued positions,[1] and that 1960s sitcoms paralleled the changing social climate in America with characters that embodied women's emerging social and sexual powers.[2]"[3] But in considering the magical powers of popular 1960s housewives specifically—Samantha Stephens in *Bewitched*, Jeannie in *I Dream of Jeannie*, and Morticia Addams in *The Addams Family*, for example—I found a disconnect between the scholarship and the visual texts. These housewife characters did a great deal of manual housework, even though they possessed the powers to avoid it altogether. When it came to housework, these characters wanted to suppress their "power" and perform as "normal" housewives. If they had any power, they appeared not to want to use it. It seemed that through "supernatural housework," 1960s television shows and advertisements actually furthered the dominant gender discourse of the 1950s—one laid bare in 1963 by Betty Friedan in *The Feminine Mystique*—which suggested that fulfillment for women involved housewifery exclusively. This disconnect between scholarship and visual texts inspired me to investigate televised housework further.

This is how the project began. My investigation of televised housework in the 1960s revealed unexpected insights, and in an effort to flesh out my discoveries, I wanted to extend my investigation to include additional visual texts, decades, scholarship, and audiences, and to understand more fully the function of housework in these texts and the relationship between television and reality. As I mentioned earlier, much of the scholarship addressing mid-century televised housework claims that domestic activities, such as housework, marginalize female characters, removing them from scenes involving important familial discussions and placing them in devalued positions. This assessment is accurate, as I can name many scenes from the 1950s and 1960s involving women excusing themselves to fill candy dishes. However, I challenge the idea that this is the primary function of these housework scenes—a conclusion that, considering I am analyzing many of these shows through a postfeminist feminist lens sixty years after their original airings, is not so surprising, as television scholar John Fiske says, "Not all viewers read television programs according to the textual strategies encoded in them.

The problem with much traditional textual analysis, whether its impulse has been ideological or aesthetic, is that it has tended to produce an authoritarian, even 'correct' reading of a text, and has tended to ascribe to the text the power to impose this reading on the viewer."[4]

As I analyze televised housework, I do so in a time when many men and women alike are choosing to leave careers and return to the home as full-time homemakers. As feminist and media scholar E. Ann Kaplan states, "childbirth and child care [are] no longer being viewed as an automatic, natural part of a woman's life cycle,"[5] and this reality allows us to reevaluate the choices made within home and family. I admire these homemaking parents, just as I do working parents, and see their commitment to the preservation of children—tasks to which housework is essential—as signifying strength. As a working parent myself, some workdays are more demanding than others. While infrequent, there are days I don't get to see much of my children, and the housework I perform for them—the clothes I clean for the next day, the lunches I prepare the night before, the ways in which I *engage in the preservative love of my children* through housework—are my only tangible methods of showing love in these moments. My working husband admits to having regarded housework similarly for years. Furthermore, I'm writing as a thirty-something, Gen X mother who has felt a disconnect with the matrophobia often identified as a byproduct of second-wave feminism.[6] I see how my own mother sacrificed for us, and if anything, I long to be more like her—I long to both preserve and protect my children as effectively and lovingly as she did, while also contributing meaningfully to my professional field. As I, like many other feminists, have come to take part in my own mothering, I realized that, as scholars Donna Bassin, Margaret Honey, and Meryle Mahrer Kaplan indicate, "our daughterly longing for mother has shifted toward an appreciation of her selfhood. The time is right to redirect our gaze and explore mother as subject."[7] Consequently, in this study, just as philosopher Sara Ruddick claims of her work on "maternal thinking," I write as much from the perspective of a daughter, as I do a mother.[8]

The lens through which I view television is informed by this reality. With this in mind, my study challenges the notion that housework functions primarily as a mechanism through which characters are marginalized, devalued, invisible, or passive, and instead proposes a different reading of housework in television, one that brings to the fore the strong, preservative, and active qualities so crucial and foundational to housework activity in both representation and reality. Using a postfeminist lens, one that both draws on and finds inadequacies in the feminisms of the past, this analysis views the performance of housework as the signification of a commitment to meet children's and family's desires for preservation,[9] a commitment that signifies, first and foremost, strength.

MATERNAL HISTORY

Even though my study involves representations of housework—not specifi-cally housework performed by women—the majority of televised housework is, in fact, performed by mothers, so a brief examination of maternal history is important to this analysis. In her book *Motherhood and Representation*, Kaplan discusses mother-related discourses throughout history, claiming they "may be described as first Rousseauian discourses, produced along with the early modern mother institution; second, Darwinian/Marxist/Freudian discourses produced along the first World War and high-modernist chal-lenges to the family; and finally, recent postmodern mother discourses, produced along with even more drastic challenges to the family through the electronic revolution and its impact on corporate capitalisms."[10] Writing in the eighteenth century, French philosopher Jean-Jacques Rousseau's discus-sions of ideal motherhood involved a new focus on the child, a routine that underscored total attention on the child, an emphasis on breastfeeding, and a regard for child-rearing as early education and lifelong preparation for adult-hood.[11] He also identified the private/female-public/male binary that would govern many subsequent discourses. Considering these ideas were similar to Puritan discourses already present in revolutionary America, Rousseau's writings, though considered radical in France, were more easily integrated into North American life.[12]

Similar to Rousseau's ideal mother as educator, in her work *Women of the Republic: Intellect and Ideology in Revolutionary America*, historian Linda K. Kerber identified the political function of mother's duties within the home in revolutionary America. "Motherhood," says Kerber, "was discussed almost as if it were a fourth branch of government, a device that ensured social control in the gentlest, possible way."[13] Mother was responsible for rearing good citizens in the private, domestic sphere, and this was articulated not only as her duty, but also perhaps the greatest way she could contribute to society and the greater good. In another well-known article, "The Cult of True Womanhood: 1820–1860," historian Barbara Welter revealed the virtues mid-nineteenth-century America believed a "true woman" should possess: piety, purity, domesticity, and submissiveness.[14] These entrenched ideologies of womanhood likely led to what historians have called domestic feminism in the nineteenth century—the ways in which women exercised strength in the private sphere, sought rights and freedoms within the home, and "made do" with the roles established for them under patriarchy.

As an aside, in some ways, there are similarities between my argument here and aspects of domestic feminism. I, too, am seeking to find new strength in the domestic activities of service performed in the home. However, my goal is not merely to give renewed value and meaning to these activities—the tasks performed by housewives who "made do" with their often patriarchally-determined circumstances—as this has been covered quite effectively by other scholars.[15] My argument seeks to apply Ruddick's concept of "maternal thinking," which I will discuss later at length—the idea that "mothering" is a practice to be performed by anyone of any gender willing to meet the preservation demands of children—to representations of housework, finding that the willingness of individuals to meet these demands through housework ultimately signifies strength.

Continuing with Kaplan's assessments of mother-related discourses throughout history, the Industrial Revolution, which resulted in the development of the small, isolated nuclear family, complete with a female homemaker/consumer and a male breadwinner/producer, who typically worked at a distance from the home while the mother maintained constant, close contact with children, and the First World War, which demanded that women enter the workforce in large numbers, are, according to Kaplan, events that affected mother and family roles in the high-modernist period in the twentieth century—a period influenced by the mother-related discourses of Darwin, Marx, and Freud.[16] These are, briefly, Darwin's survival-of-the-fittest theory, which worked to keep the mother in the home, calling for her to devote herself to the protection of her children; Marx's theories, which encouraged the elimination of the "bourgeois family," criticizing the family's ties to private property; and Freud's work, which involved unconscious childhood sexuality.

Finally, Kaplan identifies a third category of recent postmodern mother-related discourses. The Second World War, the feminist movements, social and political changes, and various scientific and technological advances, she claims, all contributed to these discourses—discourses that no longer addressed the question of *when* a woman will reproduce, but instead, explored *if* and *how* a woman will reproduce. Later discourses in the 1980s began to place the mother as *subject*. Kaplan states, "Unlike the father, who was always viewed as a subject, it is the mother's very coming into subjectivity that produces a new set of issues in culture around daycare, the combining of work and mothering, the impact of the mother's work on the child, on the father, and so on . . ."[17] My study seeks to expand this mother-as-subject scholarship, which, as Bassin, Honey, and Kaplan claim in the introduction to their work *Representations of Motherhood*, "draws on a history of feminist thought that has argued that seeing the mother as a subject, a person with her own needs, feelings and interests, is critical to fighting against the dread and the devaluation of women."[18] My study seeks to add nuance to this idea by arguing that mothers own "needs, feelings and interests" involve, among other things, the preservation of children and family, and that housework is not only a vital part of this preservation but also, from this perspective, has the potential to empower and fulfill women. Much of my argument draws on the work of Ruddick, mainly *Maternal Thinking: Toward a Politics of Peace*, seeking to apply this line of thinking about parenting to interpretations of the signifying practices of televised housework specifically.

Ruddick regards "mothering" as a practice—the commitment to meeting demands—and concludes it can be performed by anyone doing "maternal work":

> But in my discussion of maternal practice, I mean by 'demands' those require-
> ments that are imposed on anyone doing maternal work . . . In this sense of
> demand, children demand that their lives be preserved and their growth fos-
> tered. In addition, the primary social growth with which a mother is identified,
> whether by force, kinship, or choice, demand that she raise her children in a
> manner acceptable to them. These three demands—for preservation, growth,
> and social acceptability—constitute maternal work. To be a mother is to be
> committed to meeting these demands by works of preservative love, nurturance,
> and training . . . Conceptually and historically, the preeminent of these demands
> is that of preservation.[19]

Ruddick goes on to claim this willingness to meet demands does not require enthusiasm or even love. Just as mothers are not naturally "wonderful" or "good," the desire to sacrifice is not intrinsic to mothering. "Mothers, like gardeners or historians, identify virtues appropriate to their work, but to identify a virtue is not to possess it," she argues, and "When mothers speak of virtues, they speak as often of failure as of success."[20] Furthermore, she claims, maternal practice doesn't always inspire love, but rather a mix of emotions, both good and bad.[21] Maternal practice simply means recogniz-ing and responding to vulnerability with care. This is where I would like to situate my argument, as Ruddick's definition provides a new lens through which to examine the practice of keeping house in visual cultures. It explains why I began to view televised housework differently once I became a parent, interpreting the work with admiration and understanding, and why television characters, male and female, do not always seem to enjoy housework, yet still perform it.

When mothering is defined as "work" rather than an identity, the activities associated with maternal practice are not necessarily feminine activities. Film and feminism scholar Kathleen Rowe Karlyn finds that Ruddick's definition "shifts the emphasis from biology toward the work being done by people who care for children as fully human beings demanding 'protection, nurtur-ance, and training'. . . This concept nudges theories of motherhood beyond the mother-daughter dyad toward larger questions of community and ethics, governing how we care not only for children, but for the aged, and not only for the people in our immediate circle but for the planet that sustains us all."[22] With this definition of maternal practice in mind, housework can be viewed as meeting a personal need, a human need, to respond to the vulnerability of children, of community, with care, rather than abuse or abandon, and this commitment to humanity can be personally fulfilling, can signify strength, and can communicate love. This perspective becomes increasingly important when evaluating the work performed by televised housekeepers, who are depicted as being deeply fulfilled through serving a family that is technically not their own. When housework is viewed as maternal practice, it is easier to understand the mothering roles of these housekeepers, which become quite prevalent in the 1980s. I believe this perspective both imbues the activity of housework, regardless of who performs it, with the deeper significance it deserves, and establishes much-needed connections between motherhood and feminism.

MOTHERHOOD AND FEMINISM

Feminism has struggled to find appropriate and effective ways to deal with issues of motherhood, and is often criticized for never adequately addressed the *real* lives of women and children.[23] The first and second waves of feminism focused on issues of family and women's roles within it, yet many women felt disconnected from the movement because of its inability to address motherhood specifically. Media of the second wave conveyed an agenda that sought to address issues of household labor and reproductive freedom, but, as Karlyn notes, "the push to pass the Equal Rights amendment dominated the face of the movement, and the benefits of transforming the workplace did not appear obvious to white, middle-class mothers, who did not work outside the home."[24] Second-wave feminism responded to the postwar period, which, as mentioned earlier, encouraged women to return to the home, where they would rear children in an isolated private sphere, while breadwinning husbands worked at a distance in the public sphere. In response to this and Simone de Beauvoir's influential feminist work, Bassin, Honey, and Kaplan reveal that second-wave "theorists argued that mothering was the source of women's devaluation and lack of transcendence.[25] To be a person, for the most part, meant to be a person like a man. Personness and subjectivity necessitated moving beyond, or avoiding altogether, home and motherhood."[26] Examples of this scholarship include Betty Friedan's *The Feminine Mystique* (1963), which equated the home with a prison, and Adrienne Rich's *Of Woman Born* (1976), which discussed matrophobia and the feminist woman's need to break connections between mother and self.

Even more recently, into the 1980s and 1990s and the third wave of feminism, which reclaimed certain aspects of femininity and girl culture, feminism continued to struggle with the issue of motherhood. As Karlyn notes, "Marianne Kirsch charged much of the second wave with theorizing 'at a distance from the maternal' (1981) . . . Ruth Thompson wrote that feminists . . . were still failing to seriously engage with the issue of motherhood (1997). And Astrid Henry, writing from the third wave, argued that feminism has continued to undermine itself through inadequately understanding is own relation to previous generations (2004)."[27] However, many scholars have noted that, concurrent with scholarship of the second and third waves, women of color have presented a very different picture of motherhood, one that, as Bassin, Honey, and Kaplan indicate, "includes ongoing connection and recognition of the mother's social position, her strengths, and her struggles, on behalf of her family and community."[28] Scholars in the past few decades have looked to African-American mother discourses, such as those put forth by Toni Morrison and Audre Lorde, in an effort to foster a version of motherhood that underscores maternal strength. I seek to fortify connections between motherhood and feminism through a postfeminist approach by drawing on certain aspects of feminism, particularly aspects of third wave feminism, domestic feminism, and black feminism, and applying them to the activities of maternal practice, specifically housework, in forty years of television. I hope that identifying trends and inconsistencies in the signifying practices of television will reveal greater insights about the complexities of motherhood and its relationship to feminism and representation in popular culture.

MOTHERHOOD AND REPRESENTATION

Along with film and popular music, television is notoriously influential in how we view ourselves and our surroundings. Considering a large number of television programs throughout history involve various depictions of the family unit, the ways in which these shows depict familial roles, as well as the relationship of these depictions to reality, figure prominently into this study. In her chapter, "From *Father Knows Best* to *The Simpsons*—On TV, Parenting Has Lost Its Halo," marketing expert Bernice Kanner discusses the relationship of representation and reality: "Movies, popular music, and TV programming hold a mirror up to show us who and what we are—or perhaps secretly long to be, our idealized selves. The language of programming becomes our vernacular; their dress, our wardrobes; their mores, our customs, albeit sometimes exaggerated."[29] This is significant because part of my argument will involve identifying how women in reality might have absorbed and responded to televised depictions of their activities within the home in each decade, in addition to pinpointing connections of these interpretations to feminism and mother-related discourses.

The role of the mother in the media has a well-developed history of scholarship. Media scholar Rebecca Feasey states, "The contemporary media
environment is saturated with romanticised, idealised and indeed conservative images of selfless and satisfied 'good' mothers,"[30] and Kanner reveals
that while television dads were dominant, "The women were less prominent.
Loyal and loving homemakers, they revered their husbands as more important than themselves; their advice was rarely solicited."[31] Likewise, television expert Judy Kutulas mentions the centrality of dad characters, claiming,
"Mom, meanwhile, was supposed to be dad's complement, the 'steady,
loving person' who met children's day-to-day emotional needs and cooked
their suppers."[32] These scholars, among others, reveal a dominant version of
mother that is idealized as selfless, subordinate, and complementary. From
this perspective, her activities within the home, the cooking and cleaning,
are regarded as supportive to other family members' more important activities, and in order to be "good" in her role as mother, she must adhere to this
commitment to service, maintaining as much invisibility as possible. But,
as Kaplan states, what one scholar interprets as dominant will differ from
another, depending on what questions are being asked and what interests and
biases are informing the analysis.[33] Obviously, feminists have resisted this
version of mother, finding it to be "oppressive and confining"[34] and "socially
supported myth, designed to keep women in their place,"[35] but in doing so,
some feminist scholars believe the actual experiences of maternity and motherhood have been ignored or denied.[36]

Scholarship in the past few decades has highlighted this disconnect
between representation and reality, calling for semiotic approaches that
more effectively acknowledge and integrate the real-life, lived experiences
of mothers. For example, Bassin, Honey, and Kaplan situate this issue historically: "In the 1970s, feminist theory directed considerable attention to
dismantling the ideology of motherhood by understanding its patriarchal
roots and by underscoring that it did not represent the experiences of mothers
themselves. As a result, the mother's subjectivity, her ability to reflect on and
speak of experience, has become an important ingredient in altering myths
and changing social reality."[37] Similarly, media scholars Susan Douglas and
Meredith Michaels call for an elimination of "the mommy myth" created by
popular culture, claiming they are "getting increasingly irritable about this
chasm between the ridiculous honey-hued ideals of perfect motherhood in
the mass media, and the reality of mothers' everyday lives."[38] It seems that as
more feminist scholars speak from the perspective of mothers, our interpretation of mother roles and maternal practices in television are being influenced
by our own lived experiences. This is precisely the position from which
I view televised housework in this analysis. However, this cannot be accomplished effectively without at least a brief discussion of how representations

of fatherhood inform mother-related discourses and function within the framework of this study.

FATHERHOOD AND REPRESENTATION

Considering many men relinquished their roles within the home to serve in the war and then were distanced from the family in the postwar era, working long hours away from the home, scholars have noted that television shows worked to "reassert dad at the hub of the family."[39] Some, including Nina C. Leibman and Kanner, agree that promoting the father as the center of his family meant demoting the mother in response. To feminist semioticians, according to authors Sonia Maasik and Jack Solomon, the happy housewife character in general, in addition to the fact that so many shows reflected males in the titles—*Father Knows Best, Bachelor Father,* and *My Three Sons*—connoted "the interests of a patriarchal, male-centered society," rather than reflecting reality. They go on to describe this as what English cultural theorist Stuart Hall calls an oppositional reading—one that "challenges the preferred reading, which would simply take the program at face value, accepting its representation of family life as normative and natural . . . [and] proposes an interpretation that resists the normative view, seeking to uncover a political subtext."[40] I mention this because some of the points I make in this study may seem to align with those of a preferred reading, a reading that accepts at face value the televised depiction of happy housewives as reality. However, this is now such a well-developed area of scholarship that the oppositional reading has in many ways become the acceptable reading.[41]

Recent scholarship on the 1950s has focused on, what gender studies scholar David M. Earle calls, the separation of the "nostalgic image from the political, cultural, racial, and contradictory reality that was day-to-day life."[42] The actual realities of mid-century decades—the race riots, the Cold War, the large numbers of women working outside of the home, for example—are now a part of these discourses, despite the nostalgic image popular culture has maintained for some time. As historian Stephanie Coontz reveals, "Contrary to popular opinion, 'Leave It to Beaver' was not a documentary."[43] Ultimately, this scholarship indicates that the ways in which we think about our pasts are under revision, and I do not disagree with the well-established idea that television does not often reflect reality.

I propose an interpretation that resists the oppositional reading by asserting that when housework is viewed as maternal practice—as the act of preserving life—the oppositional reading must change. I'm not denying that many of these housewife characters and male-titled shows reflected "the interests of a patriarchal, male-centered society." I am arguing that focusing too much on this aspect of televised families and motherhood negates or diminishes the fact that women did and do, in reality, find joy, fulfillment, power, and strength in certain aspects of these domestic activities, and this likely informs part of a woman's—part of a parent's—engagement with these characters and shows, both then and now. To argue this point effectively, I intend to both tap and repudiate aspects of feminism, in an effort to apply a postfeminist lens to televised housework.

POSTFEMINISM

By the 2000s, perhaps in response to the increasing number of young women unwilling to identify themselves with feminism, scholars began to explore explanations for postfeminism's contradictory feminist and anti-feminist qualities. One significant contributor to this scholarship is feminist author Angela McRobbie, who explains in her work *The Aftermath of Feminism: Gender, Culture, and Social Change*, that postfeminism "seems to mean gently chiding the feminist past while also retrieving and reinstating some palatable elements."[44] As Karlyn sees it, for McRobbie, postfeminism can be understood as "less an ideology than a process by which popular culture 'undoes' feminism, while appearing to offer a well-intentioned response to it."[45] In explaining postfeminism's origins, McRobbie mentions scholars such as Jean Bethke Elshtain, who called for a type of pro-family feminism,[46] and Judith Stacey, who questioned if feminism could more fully consider parenting,[47] finding that popular former feminist writers in general were admitting, "'actually, we got it wrong,' or 'feminism did not work. It was too anti-men, too pro-lesbian, and far too anti-family' and 'this not only alienated ordinary women it also rebounded on feminists themselves by isolating them from family life and cutting them off from the pleasures of having children and from the meaningful community which emerges around motherhood.'"[48] These scholars have provided the foundational work for my study here, as I am claiming to perform an analysis informed by post-feminism because it both uses and rejects aspects of feminism. My study draws on feminism through its focus on female strength and equality within the domestic sphere, while at the same time, rejecting certain aspects of feminism by underscoring the value and strength of women serving others—of service as maternal practice. My hope it that this perspective comes through my analysis of each television show naturally, as I do not desire to create a study over-determined by the term "postfeminism." It is within this framework that I situate my analysis of housework in forty years of television.

HISTORY OF HOUSEWORK

In order to understand the importance of televised housework, the history of housework and the evolution of the housewife figure should be considered. The term "housework" originated to define household labor in the United States starting in the late 1800s, when an economy based in agriculture was replaced by an industrial one. Within an agricultural economy, certain tasks had long been deemed as belonging to men or women, but as Jessamyn Neuhaus outlines in her study on housework in American advertising, "industrialization dramatically altered both the physical tasks and the cultural meanings of tasks undertaken in the home. These tasks, newly distinguished from paid wage work, became 'housework,' thereby defining all domestic labor and care as the responsibility of wives and mothers."[49]

The determination of housework as gendered activity was shaped largely by two developments. First, as the home transformed through industrialization from a space of subsistence to one of individual consumption, families began to buy necessities instead of producing them. For example, the processes of growing one's own food and sewing one's own clothes were replaced by the activity of buying these items outside of the home, and by the turn of the century, most household necessities were acquired through purchasing. The production of goods shifted to outside of the home, and this created a new dependence on men's wages. As Sharlene Hesse-Biber and Gregg Lee Carter reveal in their study *Working Women in America: Split Dreams*, "although industrialization had a greater initial effect on the household labor of men (taking them away from the home to the factory or office), with time women's domestic labor was also affected,"[50] and consequently, this created and reinforced an ideology of binaries, of separate spheres—public and private, work and family, male and female.

Second, the advent of household utilities and technological advancements changed household labor greatly. As many studies have noted,[51] including Friedan in 1963 and Hesse-Biber and Carter in 2000, the mechanization of the home, while making most tasks easier, actually increased labor for the housewife and/or women in the family, as new "easier" ways of cleaning imposed new higher standards for household cleaning and cooking. Through the mechanization of the home, households now had stoves, vacuum cleaners, and washing machines, for example, which enabled the individual to clean more quickly and easily. Consequently, because labor could be performed so efficiently, carpets could now be vacuumed daily, sheets washed multiple times a week, and dinners cooked in a way that produced much more than just a standard single pot of stew, as was typical when households used an open hearth. The ease of household labor through these advancements also meant not only that labor increased, but also that most of the work fell to the females of the house, as the tasks men and children previously performed, such as the twice-yearly job of pulling up carpets and beating them outside, could now be accomplished daily with a vacuum cleaner by the housewife alone.[52] Thus, history presents housework as an activity that became gendered, came to be regarded as "women's work," and consequently, is vital to feminist study.

Even though visual culture largely depicted housework as the concern of housewives specifically, versus working women, as I will discuss later, in reality, housework became "women's work" whether the female worked outside of the home or not. Hesse-Biber and Carter find that the fifteen hours a week working women spend on housework beyond men, adds up to an entire month a year spent on housework. Furthermore, their study claims this problem goes beyond quantitative differences and reveals qualitative differences in household labor, as well. Tasks deemed as being "women's work," including cooking, cleaning, and childcare, are often daily and "time-bound,"[53] while "men's work," such as mowing the lawn or repairing the car, for example, are "time-flexible."[54] This means the woman is faced with performing her tasks immediately and often, while men are allowed the luxury of working their tasks into a convenient schedule. It also means that to meet these demands, women frequently perform multiple tasks at once, such as cooking and childcare, while men rarely mow the lawn and watch a toddler at the same time.

Furthermore, with regard to working women, the wage gap reinforces the division of labor in the home, as the more significant the difference between what the man makes versus the woman, the greater the difference in how much housework each performs.[55] Women who make less than men, and the wage gap means most do, often feel compelled to make up for this by doing more housework. However, households with two individuals working outside of the home and making similar wages are found to have a more egalitarian division of household labor. Interestingly, Hesse-Biber and Carter find that women who make a higher wage than males may use housework as a way to reaffirm their femininity by choosing to pick up the majority of household labor.[56] Therefore, as Hesse-Biber and Carter continue, "Housework is one of the means by which gender is strengthened, perpetuated, and created in our society."[57] Whereas this is not a study that focuses on housework ratios in actual households, I do hope to consider these points, as I attempt to understand the relationship between representations on screen and experiences in reality.

HOUSEWORK AND TELEVISION

Considering that almost thirty-five million families had television sets in the home by 1956,[58] the housewife and her daily housework schedule became a considerable influence on programming schedules developed by network executives in the 1950s. It is no surprise that the American homemaker—the person deemed responsible for buying her household products—was the primary target of television advertisers during this time, and women continue to be target consumers for advertisers even today. Networks feared the activity of housework might take away the attention of housewives from viewing television during the day. Lynn Spigel addresses this in her seminal work *Make Room for TV: Television and the Family Ideal in Postwar America*, claiming, "It was in 1951 that CBS, NBC, and, to a lesser extent, ABC first aggressively attempted to colonize the housewife's workday with regularly scheduled network programs . . . the industry aggressively tailored programs to fit the daily habits of the female audience."[59] This is significant because it reveals that the industry had housework on its mind from the beginning, and even though initially, concerns involved scheduling, content reflected these issues as well. The housewife's commitment to her housework versus watching television was believed to be so strong that networks felt she would be encouraged to watch more television if it improved the efficiency of her housekeeping. In other words, the belief was that the housewife would need labor-related motivation to participate comfortably in the leisurely activity of television. Television was considered a passive activity, so network executives wanted the programming to align more effectively with the housewife's active housekeeping schedule. Ultimately, in an effort to "create" the female consumer, the industry sought ways to connect television and housework from the beginning.

Woman's devotion to housework and efficient housekeeping is certainly reflected in television's content, which is the primary focus of this study. Muriel Cantor addresses these connections between consumerism, housework, and content, claiming, "To sell to women, corporate interests must respond to changes in women's position in society . . . Women viewers are not getting the content they necessarily want, but the content is determined by others who try to keep women as consumers."[60] Thus, in an effort to sell more household products to women, most programming that involved scenes with women also involved scenes with women performing housework. So I approach this study understanding that from the perspective of the industry, much of these housework scenes have more to do with consumerism than anything, but this study also believes the visual text in general involves much more than this, as Roland Barthes concludes, "In short, all of these imitative arts comprise two messages: a denoted message, which is the analogon itself, and connoted message, which is the manner in which the society to a certain extent communicates what it thinks of it."[61] It is this connoted message that interests me—the relationship between message and society—a subject that has received a great deal of critical attention.

The dominant discourses regarding mid-century depictions of domesticity in visual cultures tend to agree that the roles of women are often marginalized and devalued through television and advertisements. One of the seminal works in this area is Nina C. Leibman's *Living Room Lectures: The Fifties Family in Film and Television*, an astoundingly thorough examination of the roles of men, women, and children in the families of television and film in the 1950s, and with regard to housework, even though many aspects change after the 1950s, some of Leibman's observations of 1950s television are consistent with what I viewed in the televised housework of subsequent decades as well. She finds that the housekeeping activities of mother characters, particularly their duties cooking and serving during meals, cause them to be excluded from certain family matters.[62] Leibman states, "these wives and mothers are instructed that part of their domestic glory lies in [housework's] very invisibility. In this sense, the mothers are explicitly reminded to remove themselves from familial centrality . . ."[63] Similarly, Susan Douglas calls this focus on suburban domesticity in the 1950s and 1960s "television's physical and linguistic containment of women"[64] in her work *Where the Girls Are: Growing Up Female With the Mass Media*, and Spigel argues, "the woman's role as homemaker still worked to separate her from the leisure activities of her family"[65]—something occurring both in reality, as Spigel reveals, and in representation. These three authors have written stellar works in this area, and my study does not seek to disagree with them. Instead, I propose an alternative reading of housework on television. For instance, while Leibman claims women are portrayed as the "passive centers" of the home, I argue that, through housework, these women actually function as the active centers of their homes. Part of Leibman's argument involves this activity, arguing that "Mother's potential narrative and emotional dominance in the kitchen is undercut by the fact that she is always standing and serving."[66] I don't disagree with this assessment, as I, too, encounter scenes from the 1950s that seem to function in this way, but more commonly, I find housework to be the activity through which mother interjects and involves herself in familial discussion.

Even though Leibman's and Douglas's claims extend only to mid-century programming, I find that with regard to housework specifically, some aspects of televised housework are consistent in every decade. Women who watch other women keeping house in any decade would likely understand the strength behind the preservative qualities of housework—the impetus to clean house for her family involves love and a desire to preserve life, even if societal pressures, gender discrimination, and female stereotypes inform it as well. Part of this commitment involves taking care of a family in a way that doesn't demand or even require acknowledgment—the sacrifice is part of what makes her work fulfilling. Let me be clear; I am not claiming that the *housework itself* or the viewing of housework on television is necessarily fulfilling. I am claiming that female viewers likely recognize and agree that the *strength and motivation* behind the housework both in reality and representation *is* fulfilling. Those engaging in maternal practice in reality likely understand, appreciate, and even perhaps feel validated by the implicit motivations involved each time a televised housewife excuses herself from a scene to fill candy dishes, wash dishes, or fold laundry. This is the strength of the housewife that often goes unnoticed and without discussion.

This study seeks to examine televised housework through a postfeminist lens and bring to the fore the strength implicit in televised housework—the scenes both where women perform housekeeping visibly and scenes where women excuse themselves to keep house, rendering the actual work invisible—when viewed as maternal practice. These scenes reflect similar practices of women in reality, as Spigel argues, "Women's household work presented a dilemma for the twin ideals of family unity and social divisions, since housewives were ideally meant to perform their distinctive productive functions but, at the same time, take part in the family's leisure pursuits."[67] It is a fact that women sacrifice leisure time to do housework, while also making sure they participate in enough family activities so they are emotionally involved in the lives of their spouses and children. And just as I never thanked my mother for placing clean, folded clothes on the end of my bed every day, real women likely regard televised housework as reflective of the same thankless tasks of preservative love. (Incidentally, actual housework is often invisible to children in reality, a point television emphasizes in representation, especially when creating adult characters who act like children [e.g., *Silver Spoons* and *My Two Dads*]. Housework is rarely, if ever, performed in these shows.) This study argues that reading these housework scenes as marginalizing and devaluing negates the qualities of strength inherent in housekeeping.

In many scenes, television makes "visible" what has been rendered "invisible" in reality. As an unwaged activity, housework is invisible not only to economists, but largely society as a whole, and women have often been evaluated by the "invisibility" of their housework. Yet, this is an important aspect of television's contribution to this issue. As this study reveals, much of what we learn about female characters on television in the 1950s through 1980s is revealed through their housekeeping activities, making housework an integral part of television and feminist studies. In fact, Leibman finds that in certain shows, "the mother's presence is signified only by the meals she prepares and the neatness of the house,"[68] and in this way, it is the very "visibility" of mother's "active" housework that reveals her character to viewers at all. Interestingly, Spigel makes an important claim related to this issue of television's role in establishing active and passive roles:

Whereas Western society associates activity with maleness, representations of television often attributed this trait to the woman. Conversely, the notion of feminine passivity was typically transferred over to the man of the house. It could well be concluded that the cultural ideals that demanded women be shown as productive workers in the home also had the peculiar effect of "feminizing" the father.[69]

Consistent with Spigel's assessment, while the dominant discourse often regards televised housewives as the "passive centers" of their homes, through housework, I find them to be the most active members of the family—active in a way that centers them rather than removes them. I can't recall a single episode of any series in any decade included in this study where the woman in the family is depicted as enjoying more leisurely activities than the male. In fact, typically, the father will read the paper or watch television in the evenings, while the female continues her housework of sewing buttons or knitting socks.

To further this point regarding televised fathers, Leibman claims the dads in these television shows "are the most valued members" of the family[70] and that "women are not depicted as being important for the emotional needs of their families."[71] I argue that women do not need to be present for every "living room lecture" to be perceived by viewers as valued, important, and active. Repeatedly, scenes where the father alone discusses issues with children are preceded by scenes where the father discusses the issues with his wife first. In this way, the importance of the mutual efforts of couples is underscored. The husband checks his assessment with her before talking with the kids: "What should we do about the Beaver?" "Am I being too hard on Bud?" I found this to be consistent throughout. Mom doesn't have to deliver the lecture for children to know she is involved. Furthermore, mom teaches and communicates through housework. She leads by example. I mention this not to sentimentalize these activities, but to make a point regarding how viewers, primarily female viewers, likely feel validated by these depictions, recognizing their own personal strengths—a strength that preserves—in these female characters.

It is within this framework, with Leibman's, Spigel's, and Douglas's scholarship to name a few, that I initially struggled to pinpoint why popular critical assessments of televised housework and housewives did not sit well with me. I knew these scholars were accurate in their observations, but as I watched these 1950s and 1960s shows alongside my mother, as she joyfully balled my dad's socks, I felt differently about the housework depicted in these scenes. I wanted to reach a better understanding of the similarities and differences in representation and reality. Silvia Federici's book *Revolution Point Zero: Housework, Reproduction, and Feminist Struggle* brought some clarity to my reading of these visual texts and inspired part of my argument:

Even now, some of the most treasured memories of my childhood are of my mother making bread, pasta, tomato sauce, pies, liquers, and then knitting, sewing, mending, embroidering, and attending to her plants. I would sometimes help her in selected tasks, most often however with reluctance. As a child, I saw her work; later, as a feminist, I learned to see her struggle, and I realized how much love there had been in that work . . . [72]

Similarly, I recall Douglas describing related memories of how her mother would "come home from work and mop till she dropped"[73] and "was determined to have the house neat and clean at all times."[74] And then I thought about my own memories of my mother. Like Federici, most of my favorite memories of Mom involved housework, as it was the selfless, loving activity mom performed for us every day. It almost always went unnoticed; it always went without gratitude. Yet, she continued to do it, without bitterness, because it was her way of showing us love. I want this study to be reflective of this love and strength. Douglas also quotes Caroline Bird from a 1971 TV Guide article, where she states, "Television . . . does not provide models for a bright thirteen-year-old girl who would like to grow up to be something other than an ecstatic floor waxer,"[75] and to an extent, Bird is correct. Mid-century television in particular didn't exactly depict careerism for women in a positive light, but the selfless, thankless, dutiful, sacrificial work so many of our mothers did and still do is worthy of analysis, even if it is through a postfeminist study of representation and reception. Therefore, I seek to use representations of housework to highlight the strength of the female, especially as so many women presently are choosing to return to the home, not because they feel pressured to or because they can't have careers of their own, but because they *want* to. While I haven't chosen housewifery for my own life, this decision takes strength, and the daily reality of being a housewife specifically—of perpetually serving others in the preservation of children and home—requires strength for the job. This is the same strength I recognize and hope to bring to the fore in my analysis of four decades of televised housework.

I hope to avoid, however, the inference that my study is naïve, as I am aware of the validity and value of the scholarship that presently exists. Like Leibman and Douglas, David Marc mentions what he calls "housewife hubris" in discussing an episode of *Father Knows Best* in his work *Comic Visions*. He says, "Resolution of the conflict is achieved as the children learn an important lesson about the true meaning of 'winning' in life. Medals and trophies are fine, but modern homemakers (that is, modern women) are motivated by something more complex—love and the sense of duty that grows from it."[76] He goes on to claim that female characters are portrayed as needing to "learn the 'womanly' satisfactions of self-sacrifice."[77] Whereas Marc's comments and others like them view these aspects of the housewife character somewhat pejoratively—something perhaps forced upon her and certainly limiting her—this study seeks to expose the strength and value in maternal practice, whether performed by males or females. As a career-minded wife and mother, I will admit that the ways in which I self-sacrifice for my family *are* the most satisfying parts of my life, and I *am* motivated by love and a commitment to meet their demands. It makes me happy to serve them, and I believe women—people, in general—connect deeply with each other and with their visual cultures on this level. Viewing housework as maternal practice, as a commitment to meet the demands of preservation, is essential to exposing these connections.

METHODOLOGY

In this study, I analyze representations of housework in the first seasons of sixty television series from four decades, beginning with the 1950s and ending with the 1980s, a point after which the breadth of options available on television, mainly due to the "push toward mass cablization,"[78] as Marc calls it, that began in the early 1970s and gained momentum in the 1980s, makes establishing trends a difficult task. This is an important point to mention, as cable and network hegemony's influence on any television study covering these decades is significant. Marc states, "The new services brought by cable television, whatever their purposes, have become new forms of home entertainment, making the broadcast networks just three increasingly undistinguished blips among thirty-five or forty."[79] Even within this study, trends become much more diffuse in the 1980s and beyond.

I have taken a decadal approach to the organization of my study, examining the shows within each decade in individual chapters. My visual texts were chosen by referencing the *TV Guide* lists of most popular shows from each decade, including additional visual texts that I personally felt should be added, which means my methodology seeks to include roughly the fifteen most popular shows depicting American family life and/or various models of housework from each of the four decades. I used textual analysis of televised representations as an approach, searching for trends, similarities, inconsistencies, and meaning in the blocking, dialogue, character, plot, mise-en-scène, and iconography of each series.

In order to understand the way representation works, the act of creating visuals, including anything from television to advertisements, must be understood as "signifying practice." As Stuart Hall puts it in his work, *Representation: Cultural Representations and Signifying Practices*, "meaning does not inhere *in* things, in the world. It is constructed, produced. It is the result of signifying practice—a practice that *produces* meaning, that *makes things mean.*"[80] Hall uses Swiss linguist Saussure's theory to explain that meaning is never completely fixed, and individuals of a common culture must actively interpret.[81] In other words, we as a society signify and give things meaning, and as we change—as our needs change, as our knowledge changes, as our ways of communicating change—so meaning will change.[82] Furthermore, this study is also interested in the extent to which, as Roland Barthes says, representation communicates what a society thinks of itself.[83] Just as contemporary society has changed the way it regards the activity of smoking, an activity depicted in the 1950s as popular, leisurely, and healthy, representations now signify that activity as dangerous and unhealthy. For example, in one current commercial in 2014, a young girl buying cigarettes is asked to pay for them by peeling off a section of her facial skin, as the commercial seeks to signify smoking as damaging to one's health. This depiction differs greatly from the 1950s advertisement claiming "more doctors smoke Camels than any other cigarette," one that sought to signify smoking as a smart decision. Ultimately, we attach meanings to these representations of smoking, just as we do to representations of housework, and these meanings change as we change.

For this reason, my approach is informed by postfeminism, but let me first define how I will use this term for this study. I seek to expose a feminine strength that I believe is inherent in housework—a strength that works tirelessly and often thanklessly, regardless of whether her status is chosen or imposed by a male patriarchal society, because it is how she shows preservative love. My definition of postfeminism both draws from and rejects aspects of feminism, and through this lens, seeks to expose the strengths and agency of women performing housework. Whether they are housewives or working women, the strength and commitment to preservation are common to all of these individuals in all of these visual texts, and it is a form of feminism I intend to highlight. Thus, my claim is that housework signifies strength and commitment to preservation—qualities of domesticity and motherhood often ignored in standard feminist analyses of television. I am arguing that the ability of these women to put the needs of others before their own is a sign of this strength, rather than weakness, and that they are indeed fulfilled in both representation and reality through maternal practice.

It is very important, though, for me to make one point clear. This analysis does not support the idea that housekeeping is a natural attribute of being female—that females have an innate need, desire, and talent to keep house. I resist the stereotype of women being more "naturally suited" than men for housekeeping and parenting, and I understand that, as Hesse-Biber and Carter claim, "housework has come to be equated with what women are, not what they do" and that some erroneously believe "women have an innate talent for housework, enjoy it more, or have a greater need for clean clothes, household order, and balanced meals."[84] Furthermore, I resist any implication that women are better at the jobs of housekeeping and child-rearing than men, even though television depicts them as such over and over. For example, when women are in charge of their households, and the males, with regard to roles of authority, are absent, the women and their children share the housework. This is true of several 1960s programs, including popular examples *The Lucy Show*, with a household run by two women, one widowed and one divorced, and *Here's Lucy*, with a household run by a single widow. Also, in the 1970s, *The Partridge Family* depicts Shirley Partridge, a widow with five children, all of whom share in the household duties. Yet, when males are portrayed as widowers, as in *My Three Sons*, *The Andy Griffith Show*, *Mayberry R.F.D.*, *Diff'rent Strokes*, and *Benson*, or as bachelors, as in *Family Affair*, for example, they have women or family members come to their rescue to care for their home, or they hire housekeepers. The housework is not easier to accomplish for a single female than for a male, yet television depicts it as such. The connoted message, as Barthes called it, is that society expects women to continue running their homes as usual, even when they lose their husbands and absorb the added pressures of bread-winning and single-parenting, while widowed men should expect an aunt, a grandfather, or a housekeeper to move in and assume all of the household duties, so that his life remains as unchanged as possible. This trends reveals that whether television intends to or not, this contradiction implies a strength and a commitment to meet the demands of others in female characters that is not present in the male characters—a strength that takes life as it comes and, as Aunt Bee says in *The Andy Griffith Show*, "charges it in the raw." Rather than view the egregious inequality laid bare by these housework models pejoratively, this study seeks to expose the abilities of these female characters to rise to these often ridiculous and unfair expectations. More to the point, though, I am not arguing that women, in representation or reality, naturally enjoy housework, but I do argue that women, in representation and reality, find fulfillment in the preservative love that is inherent to serving others through housework.

Furthermore, I argue that for real viewers, these televised households do not signify a pressure to perform—Douglas claims that "in order to have their houses approach the standards of tidiness and cleanliness also set by these shows, [a woman] had to . . . mop till she dropped"[85]—but rather connection and common ground. I believe women recognize and identify with these aspects of service in visual representations of housekeeping, and that regardless of status, whether working outside of the home, housewife, mother, sister, aunt, or grandmother, women share these feelings for the activity of caring for family and home. In other words, it is not the housework itself that is necessarily significant, but seeing others benefit from their service that ultimately affects them so deeply. This study merely views housework as the best mechanism through which these ideas are signified.

That said, my analysis reveals roughly twenty trends established in four decades of television. Chapter 2 looks at eleven shows from the 1950s, finding that rather than marginalize the female, housework actively centers her, makes her visible, and underscores the importance of her work—the preservative love that is inherent to the work, and consequently, the strength that accompanies the choice to serve others. Housework in this decade also functions as a form of communication and often competition for female characters (e.g., *Make Room for Daddy*, *The Goldbergs*, and later *Rhoda* and *Maude*). Unsurprisingly in the 1950s, housewives are depicted as doing most of the household labor, but husbands do assist wives with housework in this decade. In fact, in comparison to the 1960s and 1970s, television depicts men as doing far more housework in the 1950s. These are usually the moments husbands and wives discuss the children. Most important, though, children recognize housework as love and approach females at these moments for emotional support. In this way, housework functions as an invitation.

Chapter 3 examines nineteen shows from the 1960s, revealing more firm trends than any other era. In this decade, television depicts men performing far less housework than in the 1950s and more shows include housekeepers or housekeeper-type characters (e.g., *My Three Sons*, *Hazel*, *The Brady Bunch*, *I Dream of Jeannie*, *Family Affair*, *The Munsters*, *The Jetsons*, and *Mayberry R.F.D.*). This is really the first decade to depict an important trend mentioned previously. When a show depicts a single male head of household, he either makes enough money to hire a housekeeper (e.g., *Family Affair*), or he has someone move in to function as a housekeeper (*My Three Sons*, *The Andy Griffith Show*, *I Dream of Jeannie*, and *Mayberry R.F.D.* establish this trend in the 1960s, and it is furthered by *Diff'rent Strokes* and *Benson* in the 1970s)—this is usually portrayed as occurring to benefit the housekeeper-character as much as the single male lead. When a show involves a female head of household, she is depicted as not making enough money to hire help and is consequently responsible for her own housework. (*The Lucy Show* and *Here's Lucy* establish the trend in the 1960s, and it is furthered by *The Partridge Family*, *Rhoda*, *The Mary Tyler Moore Show*, *Laverne and Shirley*, and *Tabitha* in the 1970s.) Also in the 1960s, television portrays women as needing to be needed through housework. (*The Andy Griffith Show*, *Mayberry R.F.D.*, and *I Dream of Jeannie* begin the trend in the 1960s, and it is furthered by *All in the Family*, *The Jeffersons*, and *Mary Hartman, Mary Hartman* in the 1970s.) In opposition to the few housekeepers of the 1950s, the 1960s depicts housekeepers as being integrated into the family, performing housework in addition to emotional support for the family. Even though the housekeeper serves the family as a family member, the housekeeper's needs and desires are rarely addressed as a family member. (*Hazel*, *The Brady Bunch*, *Family Affair*, *The Jetsons*, and *The Munsters* establish this trend in the 1960s, and it is furthered in the 1970s by *Diff'rent Strokes*, *The Jeffersons*, and *Benson*.) Furthermore in this decade, when a show depicts a single female as the head of household, her children are portrayed as sharing the household duties. (*The Lucy Show* and *Here's Lucy* establish the trend in the 1960s, and it is furthered in the 1970s by *The Partridge Family* and *The Facts of Life*.) When a show involves a single male head of household, the children do not actively participate in the housework, as these tasks are left to the house-keeper character (e.g., *The Andy Griffith Show*, *Family Affair*, *Mayberry R.F.D.* in the 1960s, and *Diff'rent Strokes* and *Benson* in the 1970s). The only exception to this rule occurs in the 1980s when the children are all female, as in *Gimme a Break!* In this case, the children share the housework, even with a housekeeper. Obviously, this underscores the gendered nature of televised housework. Additionally, when women are depicted as transitioning from being single to married within a series, they are portrayed as doing much more housework once they are married (e.g., *I Dream of Jeannie* in the 1960s and *Rhoda* in the 1970s). However, this is depicted positively, as television portrays transitioning from self-service to serving others as being ultimately satisfying.

Chapter 4 analyzes fifteen popular series from the 1970s. Most interest-ingly for this decade, television almost completely stops depicting men performing housework in the 1970s. Even when males are employed as housekeepers, their housework becomes nearly invisible in the 1970s (e.g., *Benson*). When families employ housekeepers, they become the voice of reason for the family, always offering the proper advice. However, when the housekeeper is female, this advice addresses only the private, personal, domestic realm—the female realm (e.g., *The Brady Bunch*, *Hazel*, *Diff'rent Strokes*, and *Gimme a Break!*). When the housekeeper is male, television allows him to advise also in the public, professional realm—the male realm (e.g., *Benson*, *Who's the Boss*, and *Mr. Belvedere*). This trend begins in the 1960s, but is fully developed in the 1970s. Also in the 1970s, housework is depicted as therapy for women—in this decade, many women need to perform housework to feel better about their situations—thus furthering the notion that it is ultimately fulfilling (e.g., *All in the Family*, *Rhoda*, and *Mary Hartman, Mary Hartman*).

Chapter 5 examines fifteen shows from the 1980s. Most notably, televi-sion in the 1980s responds to the egregious lack of male household labor in the 1970s by creating a multitude of shows with male housekeepers (e.g., *Benson*, *Who's the Boss*, *Charles in Charge*, and *Mr. Belvedere*). Also, the 1980s is the first decade to depict unequivocally the female who is equally fulfilled by both career and homemaking (e.g., *Webster*, *The Cosby*

Show, *Growing Pains*, and *Family Ties*). It is also the first decade to depict women as making enough money to hire housekeepers. However, in this model, the housekeeper is hyper-masculinized and the sexual interactions between the professional woman and the male housekeeper are emphasized (e.g., *Who's the Boss*). When the professional male hires the female housekeeper, sexual attraction is not depicted as an issue (e.g., *Diff'rent Strokes* and *Gimme a Break!*). The 1980s brings to the fore the issue of women performing double duty, working full-time, while still performing most of the household labor (e.g., *Growing Pains*, *Webster*, and *Roseanne*) and depicts egalitarian household management models as being most satisfying to females (e.g., *The Cosby Show*, *Charles in Charge*, and *Family Ties*). Furthermore, television in the 1980s reveals that fulfillment through serving others—through housework—can occur only when the others visibly benefit from that work. This underscores the claim that housework is fulfilling when viewed as maternal practice, as a commitment to meet the demands of others and preserve life. When those being served do not appear to benefit, television depicts housework as drudgery (e.g., *Mama's Family*). Whereas the 1960s and 1970s depict housekeepers as family members who serve the family, with no attention paid to their own needs or desires, the 1980s depicts housekeepers who are more self-centered (e.g., *Gimme a Break!*, *Who's the Boss*, and *Charles in Charge*). This self-centeredness is not depicted negatively, though. In fact, the relationships between these 1980s housekeepers and their families are depicted as being more equitable and reciprocal than the one-sided models of the 1960s and 1970s. Additionally, 1980s television calls attention to the self-reflexive qualities of television through program intros that use images of family photographs or videos (e.g., *Webster*, *Growing Pains*, *Mr. Belvedere*, *Alf*, *My Two Dads*, *The Cosby Show*, and *Family Ties*). This also connects the past to the present, and more specifically, it connects past families and their household management models to present families and their household management models.

As a final point, I want to emphasize that this study recognizes and appreciates that for many women in reality and on television, housework is considered their job simply because they are women, whether they work or not. Even females who claim to "choose" this role, often are "choosing" it because they have been reared and/or instructed that it is simply what good, responsible wives and mothers do. I also recognize that for many, this is not a choice. However, considering so many studies have done such an effective job of highlighting the marginalized, devalued, background positions of many televised women, I seek to do something different—to expose the choices to love and preserve that these women *are* making within their individual circumstances. As I mentioned at the beginning of this introduction, until recently, I never understood the fuss over housework. Now, as a wife and mother myself—and a naturally messy individual who gladly and lovingly cleans alongside her husband for two young boys—I get it, Mom. I finally get it.

NOTES

1. Nina C. Leibman makes this claim in *Living Room Lectures* (Austin: University of Texas Press, 1995).

2. Susan J. Douglas reveals this interpretation in *Where the Girls Are* (New York: Three Rivers Press, 1994).

3. Kristi Humphreys "Supernatural Housework," *Home Sweat Home*, Elizabeth Patton and Mimi Choi, eds. (Lanham, MD: Rowman and Littlefield, 2014), 105.

4. John Fiske, *Television Culture* (New York: Routledge, 2011), 45.

5. E. Ann Kaplan, *Motherhood and Representation* (New York: Routledge, 1992), 181.

6. In 1976, feminist scholar Adrienne Rich published *Of Woman Born: Motherhood as Experience and Institution*, stating, "Matrophobia can be seen as a womanly splitting of the self, in the desire to become purged once and for all of our mothers' bondage, to become individuated and free. The mother stands for the victim in ourselves, the unfree woman, the martyr. Our personalities seem dangerously to blur and overlap with our mothers'; and in a desperate attempt to know where mother ends and daughter begins, we perform radical surgery" (237).

7. Donna Bassin, Margaret Honey, and Meryle Mahrer Kaplan, eds., *Representations of Motherhood* (New Haven: Yale UP, 1994), 9.

8. Sara Ruddick makes this claim in her seminal work *Maternal Thinking: Toward a Politics of Peace* (Boston: Beacon Press, 1989).

9. I am basing this on Sara Ruddick's definition for activities of maternal practice.

10. Kaplan, *Motherhood and Representation*, 20.

11. These ideas can be found in Jean-Jacques Rousseau's *Émile* (1762).

12. These ideas are articulated in Kaplan's *Motherhood and Representation*.

13. Kerber's *Women of the Republic* (1980), page 200, is quoted in Kaplan, *Representations of Motherhood*, 23.

14. This is also discussed in Kaplan, *Motherhood and Representation*, 24.

15. For example, French scholar Michel de Certeau has discussed the tactics used by subjugated individuals or entities to subvert the dominant discourses in *The Practice of Everyday Life* (1984), and Kaplan also discusses the "tools for feminist subversion" on 25–26 of her work *Motherhood and Representation*.

16. Kaplan, *Motherhood and Representation*, 24–25.

17. Ibid., 26.

18. Bassin, Honey, and Kaplan, *Representations of Motherhood*, 2–3.

19. Ruddick, *Maternal Thinking*, 17–18.

20. Ibid., 25.

21. Ruddick is quoted in Bassin, Honey, and Kaplan, *Representations of Motherhood*, 34.

22. Kathleen Rowe Karlyn, *Unruly Girls, Unrepentant Mothers: Redefining Feminism on Screen* (Austin: U of Texas P, 2011), 20–21.

23. Karlyn discusses this on page 17 of *Unruly Girls, Unrepentant Mothers*.

24. Ibid., 17.

25. S. Ortner, "Is Female to Male as Nature Is to Culture?" in M. Zimbalist Rosaldo and L. Lamphere (Eds.), *Woman, Culture, and Society* (Stanford: Stanford UP, 1974), 67–88, is referred to in Bassin, Honey, and Kaplan, *Representations of Motherhood*, 6.

26. Bassin, Honey, and Kaplan, *Representations of Motherhood*, 6.

27. Karlyn, *Unruly Girls, Unrepentant Mothers*, 18.

28. Bassin, Honey, and Kaplan, *Representations of Motherhood*, 6.

29. Bernice Kanner, "From *Father Knows Best* to *The Simpsons*—On TV, Parenting Has Lost Its Halo," in Sylvia Ann Hewlett, Nancy Rankin, and Cornel West (Eds.), *Taking Parenting Public: The Case for a New Social Movement* (Lanham: Rowman & Littlefield, 2002), 46.

30. Rebecca Feasey, *From Happy Homemaker to Desperate Housewives: Motherhood and Popular Television* (London: Anthem Press, 2012), 3.

31. Kanner, "From *Father Knows Best* to *The Simpsons*," 48.

32. Judy Kutulas quotes Benjamin Spock (1946) in "Who Rules the Roost?: Sitcom Family Dynamics from the Cleavers to the Osbournes," in Mary M. Dalton and Laura R. Linder (Eds.), *The Sitcom Reader: America Viewed and Skewed* (Albany: State U of New York P, 2005), 51–52.

33. Kaplan, *Motherhood and Representation*, 19.

34. Ibid., 40.

35. Bassin, Honey, and Kaplan, *Representations of Motherhood*, 2–3.

36. Kaplan refers to the work of Julia Kristeva here, *Motherhood and Representation*, 40.

37. Bassin, Honey, and Kaplan, *Representations of Motherhood*, 2–3.

38. Susan J. Douglas and Meredith W. Michaels, *The Mommy Myth: The Idealization of Motherhood and How It Has Undermined Women* (New York: Free Press, 2004), 2.

39. Kanner, "From *Father Knows Best* to *The Simpsons*," 48.

40. Sonia Maasik and Jack Solomon, *Signs of Life in the U.S.A.: Readings on Popular Culture for Writers* (Boston: Bedford/St. Martin's, 2012), 12.

41. Examples of works that re-envision the 1950s include Nancy Walker's *Shaping Our Mother's World*; Joel Foreman, ed., *The Other Fifties*; Andrew Hoberek, *The Twilight of the Middle Class*; Stephanie Coontz, *The Way We Never Were: American Families and the Nostalgia Trap*.

42. David M. Earle, *All Man!: Hemingway, 1950s Men's Magazines, and the Masculine Persona* (Kent, Ohio: The Kent State UP, 2009), 13.

43. Earle quotes Stephanie Coontz's *The Way We Never Were* (29), *All Man!* 13.

44. Angela McRobbie, *The Aftermath of Feminism: Gender, Culture and Social Change* (Los Angeles: Sage, 2009), 12.

45. Karlyn, *Unruly Girls, Unrepentant Mothers*, 27.

46. Jean Bethke Elshtain, *Public Man, Private Woman* (Princeton: Princeton UP, 1981).

47. Judith Stacey, "The New Conservative Feminism," *Feminist Studies,* Vol. 9, No. 3 (Autumn, 1983), 559–583.

48. McRobbie, *The Aftermath of Feminism,* 31–32.

49. Jessamyn Neuhaus, *Married to the Mop* (New York: Palgrave Macmillan, 2011), 2.

50. Silvia Federici, *Revolution at Point Zero: Housework, Reproduction, and Feminist Struggle* (Oakland, CA: PM Press, 2012), 179.

51. In addition to Friedan's *The Feminine Mystique*, this is discussed in *More Work for Mother: The Ironies of Household Technology from the Open Hearth to the Microwave* (1983) by Ruth Schwartz and in Hesse-Biber and Carter's *Working Women in America* (2000).

52. Neuhaus does a nice job of explaining this evolution of housework on pages 2 and 3 of *Married to the Mop.*

53. Sharlene Hesse-Biber and Gregg Lee Carter, *Working Women in America: Split Dreams* (New York: Oxford UP, 2000), 180.

54. Hesse-Biber and Carter, *Working Women in America*, 180.

55. Ibid., 182.

56. Ibid., 183.

57. Ibid.

58. Leibman, *Living Room Lectures*, 3.

59. Lynn Spigel, *Make Room for TV: Television and the Family Ideal in Postwar America* (Chicago: U of Chicago P, 1992), 77.

60. Leibman, *Living Room Lectures,* 86.

61. Roland Barthes, *Image-Music-Text* (New York: Hill and Wang, 1977), 17.

62. Leibman, *Living Room Lectures,* 129.

63. Ibid., 218

64. Douglas, *Where the Girls Are*, 51.

65. Spigel, *Make Room for TV,* 91.

66. Leibman, *Living Room Lectures,* 130. This is located in the description for picture 16.

67. Spigel, *Make Room for TV,* 90–91.

68. Leibman, *Living Room Lectures,* 205. She says this with regard to *The Adventures of Ozzie and Harriet* and *Leave It to Beaver.*

69. Spigel, *Make Room for TV,* 96.

70. Leibman, *Living Room Lectures,* 172.

71. Ibid., 217.

72. Federici, *Revolution at Point Zero*, 2.

73. Douglas, *Where the Girls Are*, 58.

74. Ibid., 57.

75. Ibid., 199.

76. David Marc, *Comic Visions: Television Comedy and American Culture* (Boston: Unwin Hyman, 1989), 58 and 59.

77. Marc, *Comic Visions,* 59.

78. Ibid.,164.

79. Ibid., 203.

80. Stuart Hall, ed., *Representation: Cultural Representations and Signifying Practices* (London: Sage, 1997), 24.

81. Ibid., 32.

82. Ibid., 61.

83. Barthes, *Image-Music-Text,* 17.

84. Hesse-Biber and Carter, *Working Women in America,* 179, 182

85. Douglas, *Where the Girls Are*, 58.

Chapter 2

Televised Housework in the 1950s

The 1950s witnessed great changes regarding roles within the domestic sphere. After relinquishing previous duties, commitments, and aspirations to answer the call and go to work during World War II, the homecoming of veterans to the workforce meant many women returned to homemaking, a reality that created a great deal of uncertainty and tension in postwar America. Many women had enjoyed working and were struggling to navigate the inconsistencies between their levels of education and their often subordinate roles within the home. Furthermore, the suburbs became increasingly popular in the 1950s, an issue that further distinguished the already established binary oppositions of private/female and public/male realms. Suburban living meant the male breadwinner was typically forced to extend his distance from the home, thus increasing his time spent away from home. In many ways, housewives became increasingly isolated, caring solely for their private, domestic spheres, after, in many cases, spending years acquiring the same education as their male counterparts and, when called to do so, contributing to the American workforce in similar ways.

The 1950s also witnessed a trend to spend more time at home, as the television became common to most households. In fact, by 1956, almost thirty-five million homes had television sets.[1] Whereas families might have spent an evening going to the theater or seeing a movie in previous years, the popularity of in-home television sets placed a newfound emphasis on domesticity, thus keeping the housewife at home, in her private sphere, more often. This is something on which the television industry capitalized. Advertisers sought not just to target the housewife, but to create her as an ideal consumer—to use television to convince her of her own needs and desires for the family. Recognizing that she spent a great deal of time within her domestic sphere, advertisers found ways to improve the efficacy of reaching their target housewife consumer, such as integrating the products with the programs and using strong actresses to portray housewife characters in an effort to produce strong rather than weak consumer-characters on television and consequently, in reality. The idea behind these strategies involved selling more products, of course, but the byproduct of this focus on housewives and consumption involved a great deal of televised housework in the 1950s. In fact, much of what we learn about adult female characters in this decade occurs through their housekeeping and child-rearing activities.

When televised housework of the 1950s is examined on its own, without comparison to previous or subsequent decades, it seems initially that all female characters in these programs exist solely to perform housework and to sell products. However, comparatively speaking, when framed within a four-decade study of housework representations, 1950s television involves a great deal of housework performed by men and children. Moreover, depictions in the 1950s establish the trend of housework functioning as an invitation. Whereas this is depicted to a certain extent in every decade, it is most apparent in the 1950s that children and husbands regard the mother's housework as loving communication, as a moment when her love is most egregiously apparent, and consequently, a moment for further emotional support. In other words, 1950s television depicts mother's housework as the most popular moment for husbands and children to seek advice, support, and care. From this perspective, the 1950s establishes the trend—a trend furthered in all subsequent decades— of housework functioning as a mechanism through which family members access the love and strength of the mother characters. Rather than regarding her housework as "work that is never done," this analysis seeks to underscore mother's strength through the emotional involvement that occurs with and among her family members during and through her housekeeping duties.

Whereas this analysis acknowledges that popular 1950s television shows often present an idealized version of white, suburban, middle-class American families, completely ignoring significant segments of the population, its focus remains on popular representations of domestic labor within these models. It is important to note the significant amount of televised housework performed by the housewife alone in this decade, as the 1960s introduces more housekeepers, magic, and fantasy, thus decreasing housewife and mother-character domestic labor, and even more housekeepers are introduced in subsequent decades. The middle-class family, with the housewife at its housekeeping helm, dominates the 1950s and does not return to a similar state of popularity until the 1980s. Considering this picture of 1950s domesticity and television, this study seeks to analyze representations of housework through an approach that underscores the importance of the activity with regard to the preservation of life—as maternal practice. For this decade, my analysis includes the following shows:

The Goldbergs (1949–1956)
I Love Lucy (1951–1957)
The Adventures of Ozzie and Harriet (1952–1966)
My Little Margie (1952–1955)
Make Room for Daddy (1953–1964)
Father Knows Best (1954–1960)
The Honeymooners (1955–1956)
The Real McCoys (1957–1963)
Leave It to Beaver (1957–1963)
The Donna Reed Show (1958–1966)
Dennis the Menace (1959–1963)

THE GOLDBERGS (1949–1956)

The Goldbergs ran for seven years on television, following much success on radio. It starred writer-actress-director Gertrude Berg (Molly Goldberg) as the Jewish matriarch of her family in a tenement apartment in the Bronx. Other characters include Molly's husband Jake (first played by Phillip Loeb, then Harold Stone, and finally Robert H. Harris), her son Sammy (Larry Robinson and then Tom Taylor), Uncle David (Eli Mintz), daughter Rosalie (Arlene McQuade), and neighbor Dora Burnett (Betty Bendyke). Housework is integral to this show and is constantly visible in the Goldberg household. Molly is explicitly the active center of her family, and she runs her household quickly, calmly, and efficiently. She regularly asks for all family members to contribute and help with this work, underscoring a system of mutual efforts in household management. In the first episode, for example, Molly is returning from vacation. She immediately begins housework, telling her daughter Rosie to gather the laundry while she handles the dishes. Initially, she is overwhelmed by the amount of dishes to be cleaned, but her husband Jake begins helping her immediately. It is during this activity that Jake tells her of his latest business plan, and the scene is a rather lengthy one where they clean and discuss together. They are interrupted by the son Sammy bringing in the groceries. Molly begins unpacking and putting away the groceries, and Rosie calls for Sammy to help her with the laundry. He happily rushes to help her with the sheets. All of this occurs before Molly even has an opportunity to remove her hat from her trip. Housework serves as the signifying mechanism through which the family functions normally, lovingly, and generously to preserve the lives of others. We see and understand their relationships, personalities, roles, and closeness through these housekeeping activities. While Molly is the active center of the show, all family members share the housework, and housework is completely integrated with the action and dialogue.

Furthermore, instead of, as Leibman mentions, "specific references to Mother's omission from discussions, as she can be heard calling from the stove, 'Wait a minute, I can't hear what you are saying,'"[2] in *The Goldbergs*, it is often the father that is heard calling from other rooms, while Molly remains active and visible. In fact, it is her commitment to meeting the demands of her family that centers her, making her the most visible character in the show.

One of the patterns recognizable in this series is the use of housework as a panacea for tense or difficult situations. When Jake's conversations with guests, for example, get uncomfortable, Molly will interrupt by offering food. This diffuses the situations and is an example of how she meets her family's emotional needs through her housekeeping duties, in addition to their more obvious physical needs.

We see this in other episodes, when Molly herself is uncomfortable. She looks to housework for relief from difficult situations. For example, in the fourteenth episode when Molly becomes jealous of neighbor Mrs. Burnett for enrolling in art school, she uses her housekeeping abilities to distract and compete. The family is impressed by Mrs. Burnett's abstract painting, and when Molly feels she can't contribute to a conversation on abstract art, she instructs her daughter to set the table and tells the family to get ready for dinner. Jake mentions he admires Mrs. Burnett because she absorbs herself in cultural things. Molly replies with a very self-sacrificial response: "When you have a family, you have a family to cook for." And when her husband asks what she will do when her family doesn't need her anymore, she says, "I'll still have you to cook for, Jake." Molly's commitment to meeting the needs of her family, to preserving the lives of her family members, is depicted as her primary purpose—a commitment she takes very seriously and values greatly.

This value is revealed in how Molly uses housework to validate herself and compete with other women. When Mrs. Burnett joins the family for dinner, for example, Molly immediately tells her she must try the liver she has cooked for dinner. Mrs. Burnett begins to tell Molly how she has an art class in the morning and asks if Molly would mind picking up a pot roast, first cut, and a chicken for her. Molly begins criticizing Mrs. Burnett's choice of meat cuts and her methods of cooking, giving her advice on what cuts of meat are best and how to cook them properly. Mrs. Burnett says, "All that work just for food? What a waste of time. I'd rather be painting." Molly does not question her worth or the satisfaction she receives from housekeeping until she is made to question it by others—made to feel she should want more than she has or want to be more than she is. Molly eventually enrolls in art school and is discouraged by her inability to do it well. In trying to make her feel better, Uncle David offers to cook for her. She then begins bragging about the beautiful colors of her cooking. Her housework comforts her, and she enjoys and is fulfilled by serving, by preserving, her family. Even when pushed to do more, she returns to her cooking, recognizing the artistic qualities of the work she already enjoys. Viewing this work as maternal practice reveals the strength inherent to the work of preservation and clarifies the fulfillment depicted in female characters like Molly who are devoted to this practice.

I LOVE LUCY (1951–1957)

I Love Lucy ran for six years on CBS and starred Lucille Ball, Desi Arnaz, Vivian Vance, and William Frawley. Housework endures some interesting changes during the many seasons of this show. In the beginning, it is integrated into the comedy, and serves as a mechanism through which much of Lucy's antics occur. For example, in "Lucy's Schedule" from the first season, Ricky decides to place Lucy on a strict schedule because she is always running late. He determines what she will do at what times and for how long. Initially, Lucy appears to be "obeying" the schedule and even claims to like it at one point. However, when Ricky awakens one morning and asks where breakfast is, she claims to have already finished it. She hands Ricky a frozen fried egg because she didn't have time, according to the schedule, to cook breakfast in the morning, so she had to cook it the day before and freeze it. Frustrated, Ricky tells her just to bring him a cup of coffee. She does so, but as he attempts to stir it, he realizes the coffee is frozen, too. Lucy's housework creates the comedy, and later in the episode, this becomes even more pronounced. Other husbands want to follow Ricky's example and put their wives on schedules as well. Ricky invites the couples over for dinner, but the women have decided they don't want to be on schedules. They serve the various courses of the meal and then pick up the food before the men even have a chance to taste it, claiming, "We are on a schedule!" At one point, one of the men finds a shirt button in his water. When Lucy is questioned, she explains that she found she could save time on the schedule by washing the dishes and the laundry at the same time. Later, when she brings out the main course, the dinner is frozen because she claims there was no time on the schedule for defrosting.

Similarly, in the episode, "Lucy Wants to Move to the Country," Ricky enters the kitchen saying he does not have time for breakfast. Lucy is disappointed because she *wants* to cook him breakfast—she *wants* him to experience her fresh eggs from the country and potentially be convinced they should move to the country. When this doesn't work, Lucy rearranges the living room furniture to make the space feel too small so that Ricky will want more space, hopefully in the country. Lucy uses housework not only for comedic effect but also as a way of asserting herself and manipulating. She knows Ricky must be served, as we almost never see his character cook, clean, or get things for himself. He relies completely on Lucy for all housekeeping-related activities. Because of this, Lucy is able to use housework as manipulation. She knows Ricky would rather acquiesce than lose her service to him, and she uses this to her advantage. That's not to say that Lucy does not serve out of love. It is clear by her tolerance of Ricky's hegemony that she serves out of love. However, housework's function is unique in *I Love Lucy*, as it is an example in the 1950s of it functioning as manipulation.

What is most interesting about housework's function in *I Love Lucy*, though, is the changes it endures as the show progresses. In the first season, Lucy performs her housework very energetically, and most morning scenes involve Ricky asking for breakfast, sitting, and eating, while Lucy moves quickly around the kitchen serving him. She responds immediately to his every request in these early breakfast scenes. For example, in the episode "The Se'ance," Lucy is enjoying some leisure time in the kitchen, reading a book on numerology. When Ricky enters, he asks for breakfast and Lucy jumps up from her seat and begins serving. He sits and criticizes what she is reading, while she moves about and serves. And in "The Quiz Show," Ricky demands to check Lucy's work with regard to paying the household bills. In later seasons, however, these breakfast scenes are portrayed very differently, particularly after the birth of little Ricky. In fact, Lucy sits at the table while cooking and serving in later seasons. In the episode, "Little Ricky Learns to Play the Drums," Lucy sits at the breakfast table next to little Ricky. While seated, she prepares toast in the nearby toaster, butters the toast and gives half to little Ricky, and pours coffee for herself. All of her service is performed simultaneously with her enjoyment of breakfast. After the birth of little Ricky, Lucy is still eager to serve, but less willing to sacrifice her own needs. Interestingly, though, in these episodes, Lucy seems much happier serving Ricky than in previous episodes, where she would "perform" quickly but more out of duty than necessarily love. Later in that same episode, when Ricky enters for breakfast, he does not ask for or demand breakfast. Lucy is cleaning dishes, when she asks if she can make him breakfast, showing a genuine desire to serve. Ricky accepts her offer, and Lucy begins preparing breakfast to the beat of little Ricky's drumming on his new drum. Again, the comedy occurs through the housework. More important, though, housework functions as the mechanism through which we experience Lucy's transition from service because she *must,* to service because she *cares.* Television depicts this transition explicitly through housework.

I Love Lucy bolsters the postfeminist argument in this study because of its ability to navigate the transition from wifehood to motherhood. When housework is viewed as maternal practice, it underscores domestic strength by revealing the differences in Lucy's desire to serve before and after children. Lucy is depicted as regarding service quite differently once it becomes an act she needs to perform in order to preserve the life of her child. Her ability to recognize the vulnerability of children, respond with care, and commit to meeting the demands of family signifies Lucy's strength within this framework.

THE ADVENTURES OF OZZIE AND HARRIET (1952–1966)

The Adventures of Ozzie and Harriet ran on ABC for fourteen years and starred the real-life Nelson family, Ozzie, Harriet, David, and Ricky. The show enjoyed significant popularity on radio before transferring to television, and involved a great deal of product placement. For example, when Harriet is making cookies, her dialogue almost always involves the specific brand of cookies she is baking: "I'm just whipping up some Tollhouse cookies." With regard to housework, Harriet obviously does most of it, but those are the moments her sons come to her for advice. In recalling Leibman's claims regarding fathers being the most valued members of their families and women not being depicted as being important for the emotional needs of their families, I find that as Harriet sets the table, fills centerpieces with pieces of fruit, or folds laundry, David and Ricky approach her for advice. For example, in the episode "The Fall Guy," Harriet is arranging fruit on the table while talking with Ozzie. David enters, asking his mother where his coat is. She tells him and then excuses herself, saying "Well, I know you boys have a lot to talk about, so if you'll excuse me." This is consistent with dominant scholarship arguing these scenes marginalize the mother by removing her from the scene. However, I disagree that this is the primary function, as immediately following this, Harriet advises Ozzie on how to handle the boys. He then takes her advice and discusses it with David. Later, while Harriet is setting the table, David approaches her, asking for advice about girls and his brother. While Ozzie directly "lectures" the boys more often than Harriet, it is during her housekeeping duties that the boys see opportunities to turn to mom to meet their emotional needs. I argue that this is because the children recognize the preservative qualities of her housekeeping activities. They know the activities of mom meet their demands for survival, and they regard these moments as opportunities for additional care and emotional involvement. Furthermore, female viewers likely recognize these emotional connections over housework as well. I acknowledge that these scenes are almost never focused explicitly on Harriet's needs. She is always meeting the needs of others, but I believe mothers and parents in reality would not regard this service as devaluing, but rather would recognize and connect with Harriet's desire to preserve the lives of her children. This perspective views Harriet's work as necessary, strong, and ultimately fulfilling.

Additionally, while Harriet does most of the housekeeping, housework is often shared by the entire Nelson family. Harriet regularly asks the boys to help her set the table and then uses those moments as opportunities to ask them about their days. In the episode "David's Birthday," the parents give David a sweater for his birthday. After opening the package and encountering the sweater, Harriet takes it from him to fold, but Ozzie takes it from her and puts it away in the dresser. Housework functions as a form of teamwork in this way, and while Ozzie's contributions are minimal, housework serves as the mechanism through which familial teamwork is visibly established. The 1950s in general present a familial system focused on the mutual efforts of mothers and fathers. From a "maternal practice" position, these mutual efforts are equally important to preservation.

With regard to females being the "passive centers" of their homes, *The Adventures of Ozzie and Harriet* presents a very different picture. Harriet is constantly both physically and emotionally active regarding the needs of her family. For example, in the aforementioned episode, Harriet regularly sits and listens to her boys when they need her, but she typically notices something needs to be done in the middle of the conversation, and she begins straightening up while she is listening. Again, as I mentioned earlier, there seems to be a connection between the loving and sacrificial qualities of a woman's housework and the emotional needs of the family, as there is a pattern of using moments of active housework—setting the table, straightening pillows, making a bed, for example in Harriet's case—when the children seek her conversation and/or advice. When her housework is more passive—sewing buttons or sitting and folding the laundry—the family does not respond in the same way. I argue that family members recognize the love inherent in her work and feel most comfortable in those moments seeking more of it.

MY LITTLE MARGIE (1952–1955)

My Little Margie ran for three years on both CBS and NBC and starred Charles Farrell as widower Vern Albright and his twenty-something daughter Margie, played by Gail Storm. The series does not portray a great deal of housework, but some points are worth noting. Most of Margie's housework is invisible, and Vern or others merely refer to it, as, for example, Vern's girlfriend does so by telling Margie to throw an extra potato in the oven so she can join them for dinner. And for special occasions when they have guests, Vern insists that Margie "borrow" the neighbor's, Mrs. Odetts' (Gertrude Hoffman), maid. However, we still see some of the same patterns in this show as in other shows of the era, as well as one inconsistency. In an early episode, Vern erroneously believes Margie is pregnant, and when he encounters her moving furniture around the living room so she can vacuum, he insists she sit down and not do anymore housework. In the following scene, Vern and Margie are enjoying after-dinner coffee, referring to the tastiness of the meal Vern just cooked. This is interesting because it represents Vern voluntarily serving through housework for Margie's and the supposed unborn child's well-being, something seen in male characters of other shows, but interestingly, no mention was made of Vern's inability to function successfully in the kitchen. In 1950s television, and in later decades as well, it is a common comedic plot device to put the male in a domestic situation, where he not only functions unsuccessfully, but also continually mentions how this proves their need for the female. In *My Little Margie*, however, Vern simply claims to have made dinner to keep Margie off of her feet, and no mention was made of him struggling in the kitchen. With regard to maternal practice, it took Margie's getting pregnant, potentially introducing a child into the family, for Vern to engage in these preservative practices.

MAKE ROOM FOR DADDY (1953–1964)

Make Room for Daddy (later known as *The Danny Thomas Show*) aired on ABC beginning in 1953 and then moved to CBS in 1957. It starred Danny Thomas as the nightclub entertainer Danny Williams, Jean Hagen as his wife Margaret, Sherry Jackson as their daughter Terry, and Rusty Hamer as their son Rusty. While the show ran for eleven years with various characters and actors, this analysis focuses on the first three seasons before Jean Hagen left the show, and whereas this series generally does not have a great deal of visible housework, a few things are worth mentioning. In the breakfast table scenes when the entire family is seated eating, Margaret serves others when something is needed, but she spends the majority of the meal seated with her family. Interestingly, Danny is seated next to Rusty, who requires the most attention during meals, and Danny often serves him, tucking a napkin into his shirt to catch spills and pouring his cereal into his bowl, for example— generally preparing breakfast for his son and meeting his preservative needs. In these scenes, while Margaret stands to retrieve and serve the occasional item, Danny often performs more housework than other family members at the table.

Generally, though, housework is shared by family members. Terry offers to make Rusty milkshakes, for example, to cheer him up, and both kids help their parents with most household tasks. In another episode, Margaret decides to hire a governess to take care of the children while she and Danny take a business trip to Boston. Margaret's mother, who assumed she would be taking care of the children, comes over unannounced to stay for the week.

The grandmother and governess begin an unspoken competition over proper rearing techniques. When the governess is unable to get the children to clean the kitchen, the grandmother successfully turns cleaning into a game. It is worth noting that the cleaning is typically invisible, with characters referencing the tasks they are about to do or have already completed. But in general, whether visible or invisible, housework is either a family affair, highlighting the importance of mutual efforts, or performed by hired help.

In addition to housework, parenting appears to be shared by Margaret and Danny in the Williams household. For example, in an early episode when Danny is forced to move his son from major league baseball to the minor league, he wants Margaret to have the difficult conversation with him—a situation similar to June and Ward in *Leave It to Beaver*. Rather than Danny insisting upon having all of the important conversations with the children and Margaret functioning as his moral backup, as much of the scholarship on 1950s television claims, Danny wants Margaret to engage in these conversations. When she refuses, which she does in the aforementioned scene, Danny's conversation with Rusty turns into an opportunity for song, as he finishes making his point by singing to his son. In this way, the activities of "maternal practice" also function as mechanisms through which Danny's talent is revealed on and utilized by the show.

FATHER KNOWS BEST (1954–1960)

Father Knows Best is unique in that it is one of the only mid-century shows analyzed in the study that employs a female screenwriter early on (Dorothy Cooper). The show ran for six years on CBS and presents the Anderson family—Margaret (Jane Wyatt) and Jim (Robert Young), along with their children Betty (Elinor Donahue), Bud (Billy Gray), and Kathy (Lauren Chapin). Margaret Anderson is seen enjoying more leisurely activity than any other televised housewife of the 1950s, but most of the same patterns of housework are consistent throughout. In the episode, "Bud Takes Up the Dance," for example, when Jim reads the paper in the evenings, Margaret reads the newspaper alongside him, as she does in many other episodes. In most other shows of this decade, women knit socks and sew buttons in the evenings, while the males read. In fact, 1950s visual culture in general depicts the studies Douglas references, as she writes, "Study after study shows that while working dads have time to read the paper, watch guys with arms the size of Smithfield hams run into each other, go out with the boys for a frosty one, or simply take a nap, working moms [and I argue moms in general] barely have time—or the opportunity—to pee with the bathroom door fully closed."[3] This is part of what makes Margaret's character and housework unique. When she is seen sewing in the evenings instead of reading, she is typically completely stretched out on the couch, indicating leisure more than the physical positions of other television housewives of the era, who would often sit on the floor or upright in a chair in similar scenes. Consistent with this portrayal, Margaret is played by a strong actress, Jane Wyatt, and her character is depicted as an intelligent, confident, knowledge-seeking house-wife. She sits at the head of the table, opposite Jim, and she is the voice of reason in the Anderson household.

As with female characters in other shows, her character is revealed through her housekeeping duties. Her family, however, is less willing to help her without being asked, when compared to the Nelson family, but Margaret reg-ularly and comfortably asks for help. In the episode "Lesson in Citizenship," Margaret is cooking dinner when she asks Betty to prepare the potatoes, Bud to take out the trash, and Kathy to set the table. While these tasks seem to align with the gendered housekeeping tasks outlined previously by Federici, Margaret is consistent in asking all three of her children to perform house-work. The children do not always respond, however, and Jim is required to enforce the requests of the mother.

The children often go to Margaret for advice. In the aforementioned episode, the kids continue going to Jim for advice regarding volunteering. They end up taking Jim's advice for volunteering too literally, and Jim says to Margaret, "That's the last lecture I ever give. When will I learn to keep my big mouth shut?" Margaret uses housework in these moments to release tension between Jim and the kids. When the conversation escalates, she will often interject and tell the kids to wash their hands or set the table, furthering my claim of housework being used as a way for mothers to center them-selves and to preserve and train—points Ruddick indicates are at the heart of maternal practice. In the same episode, while Margaret prepares lunches, Betty approaches her for advice, asking, "What should I do?" This is one of my favorite scenes in 1950s television, as Jim tries to answer Betty's ques-tion. Margaret tells him not to interfere, claiming, "She didn't ask you." This is one of the unique qualities of the housewife character and housework in *Father Knows Best*. Leibman identifies that even when 1950s housewife characters ask their children questions, the children often direct their answers to the father. This is a similar situation where the father attempts to answer a question directed to the mother. Perhaps it has something to do with the employment of females on the writing team, but Margaret Anderson is com-fortable staking her claim to the emotional needs of her children, especially while she is performing activities of maternal practice. Later in the episode, Margaret even tells Jim what she thinks he should do, telling him to give a man a chance and "be a good citizen." Jim not only takes her advice, he rec-ognizes she is right and is excited to return home and tell her about his day.

When he does, he finds Margaret reading in bed—not performing housework. Again, these scenes are unique to *Father Knows Best* within this decade, as even though Margaret is still very active with regard to housework, we see her take time for herself in explicit ways that we don't necessarily see in other housewife characters.

THE HONEYMOONERS (1955–1956)

Surprisingly, *The Honeymooners* ran on CBS for only one year. It starred Jackie Gleason and depicted working-class couple Ralph and Alice Kramden (Pert Kelton and later Audrey Meadows) in their run-down Brooklyn apartment. Alice is almost never seen *not* doing housework, and considering much of the comedy of the show is the banter and disagreements between Ralph and Alice, Alice's housework is often the only explicit love shown between the couple. Despite their almost constant criticism of each other, Alice continues to cook and clean for Ralph—her housework functions as direct signification of love and sacrifice, especially when the dialogue does not. In fact, without housework in *The Honeymooners* in particular, it might be difficult to recognize the love between Ralph and Alice. I believe this is directly related to Alice and Ralph not having children in the show. The preservative qualities of housework that I'm attempting to analyze here do not exist on the same level when televised married couples do not have children. Even though Alice is still concerned with caring for and loving Ralph, partly by keeping him clean and fed, the commitment and desire to meet his demands and preserve life appears less robust and meaningful when children are not involved.

In the episode "Funny Money," Alice discusses the career, a "good job in the laundry," she relinquished to marry and be a housewife. She performs housework that is often gendered as being male tasks, such as hammering furniture. Alice repairs their furniture and even refuses to give Ralph the extra money he is requesting because she is saving to buy new furniture. She controls not just the managing of the house, but the money as well. Alice is confident, blunt, and no-nonsense, and this comes through not only in her dialogue, but her constant housework as well. Even when she merely passes through a scene, she is carrying a basket on her way to do laundry, for example. She asserts herself through her housework and runs the house with energy and confidence, but the emotional connections found between mothers and children over the activities of maternal practice in other shows are absent from this show—an observation that likely has much to do with the dynamics between husband and wife without children. This automatically underscores the significance of housework performed as maternal practice. When the preservative qualities are revealed in the activities of child-rearing and housekeeping, the work itself is signified less as drudgery and more as empowerment.

Alice prioritizes housework versus listening to Ralph and renders her household managements active and visible. In the episode, "The Golfer," as is typical, Ralph wants to share some good news with Alice, but she interrupts to tell him to take out the trash. While it seems from this scene that Alice wants to avoid having to listen to her spouse, she spends almost every scene listening to Ralph while she serves meals, cooks food, or folds laundry. Incidentally, with regard to set design, the Kramden house reflects the visibility of Alice's housework and the active nature of her management. Unlike most other 1950s family shows, the instruments and utensils of Alice's work are on constant display. The visibility of housework is advanced both through her constant housekeeping activity and through set design that renders visible the instruments that are typically invisible. This is contrary to popular criticism claiming, as Leibman does, that part of the housewife's "domestic glory" lies in her ability to keep housework as invisible as possible, consequently detaching herself from "familial centrality."[4] Alice's constantly visible housework and assertive household management places her as the active center of her family, and her love for Ralph is almost solely revealed through these activities.

The Honeymooners also directly addresses the contemporary scholarship regarding housework in reality, as well. In describing the housewives of this era, Douglas writes, "Between cleaning, making Jell-O molds, being den-mothers, chauffeuring, running the nation's PTAs, and ironing Dad's boxers, housewives in this period averaged a 90-hour work week.[5] Yet ads for household appliances, like Maytag's, which showed an ecstatic woman gushing, 'Look . . . no work!' or the one for an electric mixer that instructed, 'You Dial It!—Dormeyer Does It!' suggested that women led a life of leisure."[6] Alice addresses often the idea that "a woman's work is never done." In the episode, "A Woman's Work Is Never Done," Alice is busy setting the table, when Ralph chides her for not laundering his bowling shirt that day. She didn't get to it because she was busy doing other housework. Then, he scolds her for not sewing his socks, and asks her for her excuse, claiming she has been fooling around all day. Alice goes through the drudgery of her day, detailing her housework, and sarcastically claiming the work is "such fun" because of all of her "modern conveniences." Ralph demands that he is going to begin giving her demerits when she doesn't do what he asks, but Alice responds by reminding him that while his work day is eight hours, hers is twenty-four: "Man works sun to sun, but woman's work is never done." This points toward important housework-related discourses of the era.

Consequently, Alice demands they hire a maid and decides to return to work. Ralph is embarrassed that Alice is working, but he acquiesces and they go through four maids in a week, all quitting because Ralph is difficult. In an effort to hide this, Ralph dons an apron, mopping and cleaning the house himself. Furthermore, he hires a friend to help him, but the friend refuses to do certain tasks, such as washing dishes—tasks he considers to be "women's work." Ultimately, the duo end up ruining Ralph's beloved bowling shirt through their inability to iron properly, leaving Ralph to claim, "This kind of work isn't for a man; this is woman's work." Alice responds, "You found out housework is a lot harder than you thought," and she makes Ralph admit that housework is harder than his job. As with other television housewives, plots are rarely about Alice's needs, and her character spends most of her time serving Ralph's physical and emotional needs. That said, this episode functions to further the idea that viewing housework as maternal practice is essential to it being understood as fulfilling activity. Since the preservative qualities do not seem to be inherent in Alice's work, the work does not appear to fulfill her, even if it still functions to signify a commitment to meeting the demands of marriage.

THE REAL McCOYS (1957–1963)

The Real McCoys aired on ABC and then CBS for six years, and depicted the lives of the McCoy family, after moving to California from West Virginia. Family members include Grandpa Amos McCoy (Walter Brennan), his grandson Luke (Richard Crenna), Luke's young wife Kate (Kathleen Nolan), his teenage sister Hassie (Lydia Reed), and his younger brother, Little Luke (Michael Winkelman). In *The Real McCoys*, housework often functions as a factor for determining the quality of a woman, and unlike other shows of its era, the rural lifestyle of the McCoys blurs the gendered distinctions typically seen in housework. Women will work both inside and outside of the home, maintaining the standard duties of cooking and cleaning, but also attending to animals. In the episode "California, Here We Come," Grandpa chides Luke for not marrying the 16-year-old girl who "can lick two men in the morning and plow in the afternoon," and for taking up "with a skinny woman past twenty who sat right there and bold as brass said she didn't know how to shoe a mare." Grandpa associates a woman's ability to work equally well both in the house and on the land with quality as a person and as a family member contributing to the unit as a whole. Grandpa claims, "Some women is workers and some not." The ability and willingness of a woman to work is of primary importance to him, and even though this show departs from others with women working the interior and exterior, it underscores the importance 1950s television placed on roles and mutual efforts of individuals in those roles.

Interestingly, issues of gendered work inside and outside of the home are the basis of most of the arguments between Grandpa and his family, as we see old traditions being traded for new ways of thinking. We still see females young and old, serve and work more than males, making them more active than passive: they sew garments, repair Grandpa's furniture, wash dishes, and garden. But while, initially in the series, Grandpa makes it clear, especially in his dealings with his female neighbor, that he does not have much respect for women, this begins to change. Grandpa makes fun of Luke for listening to his wife, claiming a man who listens to his wife is a puppet. Luke not only listens, but he also takes her advice and acts upon it. In this regard, Kate does not function merely as his moral backup, but as his partner, and her status as such is revealed as she begins to adopt more housekeeping abilities. This presents an interesting model of equality between male and female occurring with the increase in housework. The female characters in the show seem unaffected by Grandpa's lack of respect for them and their work. They continue to serve, and through these activities—fixing his chair, serving him warm milk, for example—Grandpa develops a respect and appreciation for these women even if they still can't "shoe a mare."

Like Alice and Ralph in *The Honeymooners*, Kate and Luke are married without children, but Kate's housework is depicted as loving and fulfilling, much like other 1950s television families with children. Recalling Karlyn's assessment that Ruddick's definition of maternal practice "nudges theories of motherhood beyond the mother-daughter dyad toward larger questions of community and ethics, governing how we care not only for children, but for the aged," it seems that Kate's desire to preserve Grandpa's life is what makes her service appear more loving and fulfilling than Alice's work for Ralph in *The Honeymooners*. This reinforces the importance of evaluating housework from this perspective.

Furthermore, in *The Real McCoys*, housework functions as the mechanism through which binaries, young and old, male and female, and traditional and modern find common ground. The females in this show in particular reflect a strength that persists even without respect or acknowledgment, and as with other shows, it is these moments of preservative love inherent in their housework that Grandpa finds opportunities for connection and change. Consequently, the show highlights the value of roles and of mutual efforts among family members.

LEAVE IT TO BEAVER (1957–1963)

Leave It to Beaver ran on CBS and then ABC for a total of six years and portrayed the Cleaver family: June (Barbara Billingsley), Ward

(Hugh Beaumont), older son Wally (Tony Dow), and Theodore "Beaver" Cleaver (Jerry Mathers). This situation comedy focuses on middle-class, white American boyhood, and like *Dennis the Menace*, most of the comedy centers on Beaver's well-intentioned mischief. Housework and the housewife character change as the series develops, though, so this analysis will focus on the early episodes, which involve a more egalitarian approach to housekeeping in the Cleaver household. In the episode "Beaver Gets Spelled," for example, the family is seated eating dinner, when both parents ask the boys about their days. The boys respond to their parents equally and then ask to be excused. June begins clearing the table, but when she tries to take Ward's dishes, he stops her and says, "I'll get that." In fact, in these early episodes, Ward helps June quite a bit with the housework. In the same episode, he washes dishes with her, as they discuss Beaver's latest problem. As another example, in the episode "Captain Jack," June finds Ward cleaning out the junk from under the couch cushions in the living room. In general, in these early episodes, a great deal of the housework is accomplished through the mutual efforts of June and Ward, indicating a shared commitment to preservation.

One criticism about these scenes, though, is the assessment Mary Beth Haralovich makes regarding the character of June. She finds that June is always at a loss about why her boys act the way they do,[7] always looking to Ward to explain the boys' behavior to her. I find this assessment to be accurate, as in these moments when June and Ward perform housework together, June asks unnecessary questions, much like a child. In the aforementioned episode, Beaver is hiding in a tree to escape what he believes is going to be punishment for having a note sent home from his teacher. He tells his parents that he plans to stay up in the tree until he dies. Later, while they are washing dishes together, June asks, "Ward, do you think Beaver really would have stayed up there until he died?" Obviously, this is not a question many mothers would actually feel the need to ask, and this, along with other similar questions, contributes to the assessment that June is often portrayed as relying on Ward for parenting instruction and advice.

With regard to the idea that, as Leibman claims, an "analysis of power configurations in television reveals that women are not depicted as being important for the emotional needs of their families,"[8] I find that in the early episodes of *Leave It to Beaver*, June actually talks more with her boys than Ward. She may still go to Ward for explanations about their behavior, but she is very involved, both through dialogue and blocking, in the emotional needs of her children. Dialogue often makes explicit their sharing of the parenting duties. One example of this is found in the episode "Captain Jack," again. In this episode, the Cleavers have a maid, Minerva, who comes three times a week to help with cleaning and laundering. This alone is unique to the 1950s televised household, as the 1950s housewife is rarely portrayed as having hired help.

However, June does in this episode. The boys have purchased a small alligator and are keeping it hidden in the basement. When Minerva discovers it while doing laundry and tells Ward, he believes she is drunk and fires her. Later, when Ward and June need to talk with the boys about getting rid of the alligator, Ward asks June to talk with them. She refuses because she was already the one to apologize to Minerva about the misunderstanding. This scene is significant because it shows the male actually requesting the female to discuss important issues with the kids, instead of the pattern Leibman describes in claiming that June often misses important discussions occurring between father and sons because she is in the kitchen.[9] Leibman's description is accurate in later seasons, but in early episodes, Ward asking June to have the important discussion with the boys, instead of doing it himself, represents an ideology that is less patriarchal hegemony and more egalitarian. Parenting is depicted as being shared and the male has confidence in mother's ability to parent effectively, regarding her as more than just his "moral backup."[10] Ward often asks June, "Where are the boys" or "What are the boys up to," and she almost always knows. In this way, she is actually more involved than Ward, and considering the great deal of housework performed by June, it is likely her constant housework around the house makes her aware of the boys' activities. This, again, ties housework directly to the emotional, preservative needs of her family by positioning June in an actively centered role.

It is important to mention how housework also contributes to the physical relationship between June and Ward. While June is washing dishes or cooking, Ward will often come up behind her and place his hands on her waist or embrace her from behind. There is a clear physical attraction that occurs over housework in these early episodes that isn't as prevalent later on, and it seems to indicate the communicative love I argue is inherent in these acts of domestic service. It is also in these moments that June tells Ward to, "Go tell the boys to wash up for dinner." The instruction comes from the female to the male, and Ward always responds happily. In these ways, the early episodes of this show resist the patriarchal hegemony so often ascribed to the Cleaver family. Furthermore, June's and Ward's "maternal practice," housework specifically, is directly connected to love, both emotionally and physically, between family members in the Cleaver household, and functions as a signifier of care, desire to preserve, and in many scenes, equality.

THE DONNA REED SHOW (1958–1966)

The Donna Reed Show, which ran for eight years on ABC, reveals the lives of the Stone family, including housewife Donna Stone (Donna Reed), her pediatrician husband Alex Stone (Carl Betz), their daughter Mary

(Shelley Fabares), and son Jeff (Paul Petersen). As with similar shows of
the decade, Donna performs most of the housework. She functions as the
active center of her home through her housework, and she contributes to
the emotional well-being of her children, making decisions about their rearing alongside her husband. One thing that is unique about this show is the
number of narratives centered on Donna. In the plots of most shows of this
era, Leibman and Douglas are accurate that women assume background
positions. Even though housework functions to bring them to the fore within
individual scenes, plots are rarely about the needs of these housewife characters. *The Donna Reed Show*, however, often addresses Donna's needs and
desires, outside of maternal practice. In the episode "Pardon My Gloves,"
for example, Donna is preparing to star in a play. This plot point is revealed
through her housework, as she practices her lines while serving her family
breakfast. She is actively moving around the table, serving, while the family
talks with each other, but the subject of their conversation is Donna and her
play. They ask her to perform for them and she does so while serving eggs.
This activity functions as a unique blurring of binaries, as Donna is simultaneously serving and receiving attention.

Furthermore in this episode, Donna's need to rehearse requires that Alex
and the kids take care of the housekeeping duties while she is away. In one
scene, Alex puts on an apron and unsuccessfully tries to cook dinner. "Maybe
tackling dinner wasn't such a good idea after all," he says as he clumsily
pours a mixture into a bowl. After tasting it, he states, "Now, I'm convinced."
Initially, this scene seems inconsistent with my argument, as it is yet another
scene where the father figure—an individual not only capable of cooking
successfully, but one who likely did so regularly before marrying—fails at
housekeeping in order to highlight how much they "need" the mother figure
to perform these tasks for them. Hesse-Biber and Carter find that, in the
evolution of housework as "women's work," through visual culture, "women
were shown as naturally suited for housework and men for employment,"
and that "today, we can witness vestiges of this ideology in some men's
comments about the 'natural talent' of their wives or companions for doing
laundry or washing the dishes."[11] Plots that further this approach are common in the 1950s, and this episode is a good example of this. The reason
I include it here is because of the insistence by the children that they figure
out how to take care of themselves and not eat out because they don't want
to make Donna feel she is neglecting them for the stage. In other words,
Donna's self-sacrificing qualities are so apparent and such a defining aspect
of her personality that her family knows she will stop any self-serving activity if it supersedes her self-sacrificing. In order for Donna to continue doing
something for herself, the family must convince her they are able to be self-
sufficient—they are aware of her intense desire to preserve through activities

of service. Housework signifies love and self-sacrifice from both Donna and the rest of her family. Following these statements in this episode, Donna rushes in and quickly cooks dinner, while the family sit at the table and listen to her talk about the play. This study views Donna as the active center of her family, advancing a function of housework as a mechanism that signifies preservative love and emotional connection among family members. Housework is how they communicate these feelings and the commitment to meet each other's needs.

Donna's desire to star in a play also serves as a unique emphasis on the leisure activities of the housewife character—something 1950s shows and criticism rarely address. Like Margaret Anderson of *Father Knows Best*, Donna enjoys leisurely activities alongside her husband, as she does in the episode "Weekend Trip," when they kiss in front of the fire at the end of the day. Alex helps her with housework, often drying dishes after dinner while discussing the kids. Just as Alex frequently takes on housekeeping tasks gendered as female activities, Donna participates in tasks often deemed as belonging to males. In the same episode, Jeff is being teased at school and eventually comes home with a black eye. Donna takes him into the backyard, dons boxing gloves, and attempts to teach Jeff how to defend himself. Compared to other examples of the decade, housekeeping and child-rearing are considerably shared in the Stone household, and activities are often gendered less obviously than in other shows. This indicates the desire of both mother and father to preserve the lives of their children is made explicit in this show through a domestic realm that is more egalitarian and shared than in other examples, where the domestic realm is depicted very clearly as a female realm.

DENNIS THE MENACE (1959–1963)

Dennis the Menace aired for four years on CBS and featured the Mitchell family: Alice (Gloria Henry), Henry (Herbert Anderson), and Dennis (Jay North). This is another show that uses a female cowriter early in the series (Peggy Chantler Dick), something not necessarily typical in the 1950s, and plots revolve around Dennis's mischief, even though he is a well-meaning boy. In fact, much of the show's comedy occurs when Dennis gets in trouble while his parents aren't looking because they are engaged in housework. That's not to say that the parents are removed from scenes to perform housework or that the housework is invisible. Dennis's mischief is often revealed during housework. For example, in the episode "Dennis Goes to the Movies," Alice is making Dennis's bed, but when she can't get it just right, she pulls back the covers to reveal a large stash of toys Dennis has clearly been collecting in his bed. In another scene, Dennis has unscrewed a leg of the kitchen table and asks his friend Joey to hold up the table in the meantime. Alice is trying to cook in the same space, so she tells the boys to go play outside. Dennis tries to explain why they can't run outside, but Alice does not look up from her cooking. She continues to work while she talks to them. Dennis and Joey obey by rushing outside, and the table comes crashing down. Alice is very involved with Dennis, but her housework is often the reason she does not see the full extent of his activities. At the same time, *Dennis the Menace* emphasizes the preservative qualities of housework when viewed as maternal practice, as a great deal of Alice's work within the home involves her performing tasks that are explicitly protective, safeguarding Dennis from his own actions.

Interestingly, in this series especially, housework is performed regularly by females *and* males. In the same episode, Alice asks Henry to take her to a movie. First, it is interesting to see the mother show such a strong desire for leisure apart from her children. Dennis is more mischievous than other television children, so mother's desire to get away adds to the comedy, but still, it is a focus on mother's leisure—activities also present in *Father Knows Best* and *The Donna Reed Show*—that scholarly criticism doesn't often address in shows of the 1950s. Alice and Henry hire a babysitter, and in preparing for the babysitter's arrival, Alice says, "Oh, the living room's a mess. We'd better straighten it." In most other shows of the 1950s, the dialogue would have involved the housewife saying, "*I'd* better clean it," but not only does Alice, in a way, tell Henry to help her, they both immediately rush into the living room, get on their hands and knees, and begin picking up the room.

Both characters do housework, and both use housework as a way of showing preservative love for Dennis and each other. In fact, almost every time we see Alice doing some form of housework, Henry is doing another form of housework. In the episode, "Dennis and the Signpost," for example, Dennis yells over the fence to his mother, "Whatcha doing, Mom?" She says she just finished sweeping the patio and dad is cleaning out the attic. This dynamic also extends to the neighbor couple, George and Martha Wilson (Joseph Kearns and Sylvia Field). While Martha is cooking, she regularly asks George to complete tasks, such as feeding the dogs, painting the house, working in the garden. Their housework is actually quite visible, as these are the most common moments for Dennis to approach Mr. Wilson and, consequently, cause trouble for him. Still, the housework serves a similar function as it does in other shows. Since it signifies love and service, even between neighbors, it is the center of the action, whether that action involves seeking advice or getting into trouble. Furthermore, the sacrificial qualities of housework in the show make Dennis's antics all the more endearing. He is often trying to "fix" things for people, as he does in the episode "The Fishing Trip," where he attempts to cook and makes a mess, or in the episode "Dennis Goes to the Movies," where he wants to repair the kitchen table. Dennis wants to return the love he recognizes in the housework of his parents, yet he can't ever seem to get it right and that creates the comedy of the show. *Dennis the Menace* contributes significantly to this study, as, in a unique way, it depicts the preservative love Ruddick describes of maternal practice from both parent and child. Dennis's desire to care for his parents, like their desire to protect and preserve him, is made explicit through his constant well-meaning domestic mishaps.

CONCLUSION

Ultimately, analyzing housework in these eleven popular shows of the 1950s reveals several patterns, signifies certain meanings, and exposes inconsistencies with present scholarship. First, there is the claim that "men never attempt any of the chores on their own, nor do they assist in any other type of household work it is indeed, only the husband's participation in the relatively minor tasks of before- and after-dinner duties that allows the husband and wife to discuss family problems . . ."[12] My study found Ward Cleaver (*Leave It to Beaver*) voluntarily clearing the table and cleaning out couch cushions, Ozzie Nelson (*The Adventures of Ozzie and Harriet*) putting away his son's clothes, Ralph Kramden (*The Honeymooners*) mopping and cleaning after the maid quits, Alex Stone (*The Donna Reed Show*) cooking dinner for his family while his wife rehearses for a play, Henry Mitchell (*Dennis the Menace*) picking up the living room and cleaning out the attic, Danny Williams (*Make Room for Daddy*) preparing breakfast for his son, and Vern Albright (*My Little Margie*) cooking dinner for his daughter. In each show, these activities are performed voluntarily by men without the request of the female, thus signifying the importance of mutual efforts in familial models of the 1950s.

This raises another point. Through these domestic duties, the male characters take on certain traits that have historically been feminized, thus, in a way, breaking down what Leibman identifies as the "strict oppositional construct in which men and boys are associated ideally with strength, intelligence, logic, consistency, and humor, while women and girls are rendered intuitive, dependent, flighty, sentimental, and self-sacrificing."[13] This study recognizes self-sacrifice and strength as being synonymous, as strength is, in a way, required to self-sacrifice. The males and females of these shows often represent the qualities of strength and self-sacrifice equally, a point that reinforces my argument that real housewives of the era would have connected with the strength and partnership they saw in the characters, rather than identify mother's housekeeping duties and father's authoritative parenting as byproducts of patriarchal hegemony.

Furthermore, analyses of 1950s television have also claimed these images depict women as not "being important for the emotional needs of their families," that their value is found in being the "passive centers" of the home, and that their "presence is signified only by the meals [they] [prepare] and the neatness of the house."[14] This study challenges these assessments, as consistently, I see children approach their mothers for advice while the females are performing housework, thus connecting the inherent love in housekeeping to the child's emotional need for preservative support. I witnessed often males requesting females to discuss important topics with children, representing a desire to share these parenting duties—sharing both the challenges and the rewards. In general, females are in constant, active motion through housework, making them far from passive, but rather active, centered, and emotionally involved. And fathers almost always approach the females first before making any parenting decisions, rendering them not as "moral backups" but as moral centers of the home.

The aspects of housekeeping 1950s housewives likely found most fulfilling are the same strength and drive to preserve depicted in these shows. Thus, if we apply Roland Barthes' theory that the connoted messages of these televised images is "the manner in which the society to a certain extent communicates what it thinks of it,"[15] and Hall's determination that "meaning does not inhere *in* things, in the world. It is constructed, produced. It is the result of signifying practice—a practice that *produces* meaning, that *makes things mean*,"[16] we must conclude that society of the 1950s likely regarded preservative love, strength, and sacrifice as inherent qualities of housework, whether performed by males or females. We must also conclude that based on televised representations of housework, 1950s society regarded females as emotionally invested in their families, partners in parenting, and actively centered within the familial structure. In this way, as we perform the signifying practice of "making things mean," we construct a function of housework in 1950s television that is not marginalizing, but rather centering, that is not devaluing but rather enhancing, that is not passive-making, but rather active-making, that does not view service as a sign of weakness, but rather of strength, and lastly, that does not view caretaking as limiting, but rather fulfilling. This perspective—evaluating housework as the maternal practice of recognizing vulnerability and meeting needs—allows us to use aspects of feminism—the ways black feminism recognizes mother's strengths and struggles and domestic feminism acknowledges the importance of women's domestic work, for example—to navigate the issue of motherhood. This postfeminist stance is important to understanding how 1950s visual culture may have reflected the actual lives and sentiments of real women, how women may have received and informed these visual texts, and how contemporary feminism can effectively engage issues of motherhood, past and present.

NOTES

1. Leibman, *Living Room Lectures,* 3.
2. Ibid., 130.
3. Douglas, *Where the Girls Are*, 59.
4. Leibman, *Living Room Lectures,* 218.
5. The two classic studies of women and housework are Ruth Schwartz Cowan, *More Work for Mother: The Ironies of Household Technology from the open Hearth to the Microwave* (New York: Basic Books, 1983); and Susan Strasser, *Never Done: A History of American Housework* (New York: Pantheon, 1982).
6. Douglas, *Where the Girls Are*, 54.
7. Mary Beth Haralovich, "Sitcoms and Suburbs: Positioning the 1950s Homemaker," *Quarterly Review of Film and Video* 11, no. 1 (May 1989), 79.
8. Leibman, *Living Room Lectures,* 217.
9. Ibid., 130.
10. Ibid., 118.
11. Hesse-Biber and Carter, *Working Women in America*, 179.
12. Leibman, 220.
13. Ibid., 174.
14. Ibid., 217, 197, 205. Leibman says this with regard to *Leave It to Beaver* and *The Adventures of Ozzie and Harriet* specifically.
15. Barthes, *Image-Music-Text*, 17.
16. Hall, *Representation*, 24.

Chapter 3

Televised Housework in the 1960s

The 1960s witnessed a great deal of change and unrest, as it was the decade of the civil rights movement and the Vietnam War, in addition to second-wave feminism. At the time, as we saw with most female television characters of the 1950s, a woman's proper and most fulfilling place was considered to be in the home, but in 1963, Betty Freidan published *The Feminine Mystique*, a groundbreaking work that changed the way society viewed the roles of women. In my work "Supernatural Housework: Magic and Domesticity in 1960s Television," I discuss the connections between Friedan's text and 1960s supernatural television specifically,[1] and it is worth mentioning it here as well, as it is plausible that the increase in televised housework performed in the 1960s could in part be a result of the influence of this work. Certain shows discussed in this chapter, such as *The Patty Duke Show*, include episodes that could arguably be direct responses to some of Friedan's claims. Friedan describes the "problem that has no name" as the common boredom of the American housewife during the 1950s. She addresses the inconsistencies between the educational levels women had attained and the educational level required to perform housework—a reality Friedan claims left women restless, bored, and ultimately, bewildered that housewifery hadn't fulfilled them in the ways they expected. By the 1960s, housewife boredom had become a national issue. Friedan's work is perhaps one of the reasons 1960s television actually depicts more women performing housework and fewer men involved in domestic duties than the 1950s—housework in general as gendered activity had become a part of the dominant gender discourse of the 1960s.

1960s TELEVISION, WAR, POLITICAL MOVEMENTS, AND THE BORED HOUSEWIFE

With regard to the change, unrest, and exposure of housewife boredom in the 1960s, television answered the call. David Marc discusses television's response to societal changes in his work *Comic Visions*:

> As the 1960s hit civil rights and Vietnam in high gear . . . the networks sought to retain as high a degree of least-objectionability in this polarized atmosphere as possible. The sitcom, a representational art committed to harmony and consensus, found refuge in visions of America's premetropolitan past and fantasies of witches, genies, and nannies who could do the vacuuming by magic.[2]

This "high degree of least-objectionability" was often captured through variety and ambiguity, and this was accomplished in two ways: First, even though the 1960s involved many shows centered on fantasy and magic, as Marc mentions, this decade also maintained a great number of shows furthering trends established in the 1950s—shows that did not involve the fantastic elements, but rather presented typical, "traditional" American family-centered plots. The combination of past with present trends serves as an example of how networks sought to deal with a changing social climate through variety.

Second, 1960s television witnessed characters, especially female characters, with ambiguous desires, who could have it all—who could potentially enjoy both sides of the various ideological binaries (e.g., public and private, domestic and career, natural and supernatural, real and fantasy, etc.). For example, Friedan identifies the essence of housewifery as the elimination of "women's creative energy, rather than using it for some larger purpose in society,"[3] but many 1960s housewife characters did not have to suppress their creative impulses because they had the power to act on them. For Douglas, it was this ability to act on creative ideas that separates the 1960s televised housewife from the real-life housewife, as she discusses in her analysis of the character Samantha Stephens from the popular television series *Bewitched*: "Samantha has a more exciting destiny. While she claims that marriage to Darrin is what she wants, she gets to have it both ways, to have the reassurances of being a suburban wife and the adventures of being a more unconventional woman."[4] Samantha enjoys multiple roles and dips into multiple sides of various binaries. Her character is an example of how Freidan's text and second-wave feminism shook up preconceived notions of women's roles and/or desires, and in general, how 1960s television, in response to war and political movements, focused on the fantasies and daydreams of men and women alike.

Television, according to Marc, responded with characterizations that were devoted to escapism:

But during the 1960s, faced with more cultural ambiguity than the genre dared handle, the sitcom went into what might be called a period of "deep escapism." If the suburb-realist domesticoms of the 1950s had strived to portray a vision of the "likely," the next generation of sitcoms, including shows such as *The Beverly Hillbillies* and *Gilligan's Island*, seemed utterly indifferent to verisimilitude, preferring instead to explore and allegorize the turgid daydreams of American mass culture[5]

In other words, 1960s television chose to deal with the real through images of the unreal. Spigel finds that these escapist shows "provided a cultural space in which anxieties about everyday life could be addressed, albeit through a series of displacements and distortion."[6] The changing social climate of the 1960s—one that involved the women's and the civil rights movements—is reflected in the combination of visual texts maintaining 1950s trends and texts reflecting the qualities of magic, fantasy, and fortune.

My analysis is concerned specifically with representations of housework within this framework. Regarding 1960s televised housewife characters specifically, scholars have addressed their housekeeping tasks as being moments in 1960s television when supernatural abilities are often exposed. Scholars, such as Douglas, view this as "domesticating the monster"—acknowledging the "impending release of female sexual and political energy, while keeping it all safely in a straitjacket."[7] Like Douglas, popular interpretations of the supernatural housewife characters of the 1960s claim that the fear of these supernatural powers, or sexual energy, remaining uncontained caused male characters to demand that their women not use their powers, and if they must, they should confine their powers to completing domestic chores within the private sphere.[8] If the televised housekeeping tasks of the 1950s had been perceived as boring, as some have suggested,[9] in the 1960s, the boring is transformed into the thrilling. Interestingly, though, while this decade presents numerous shows comprising fantasies, daydreams, magic, and good fortune, in addition to the number of shows maintaining the trends of the 1950s, this study finds that representations of housework are consistent with other decades in functioning as signifiers of preservative love and ultimately strength, in addition to serving as moments for emotional connection and active centering. This chapter seeks to underscore this strength by analyzing representations of housework as maternal practice within the following nineteen shows:

My Three Sons (1960–1972)
The Andy Griffith Show (1960–1968)
Hazel (1961–1966)
The Dick Van Dyke Show (1961–1966)

The Beverly Hillbillies (1962–1971)
The Lucy Show (1962–1968)
The Jetsons (1962–1963)
The Patty Duke Show (1963–1966)
Petticoat Junction (1963–1970)
Gilligan's Island (1964–1967)
Bewitched (1964–1972)
The Munsters (1964–1966)
The Addams Family (1964–1966)
Green Acres (1965–1971)
I Dream of Jeannie (1965–1970)
Family Affair (1966–1971)
Here's Lucy (1968–1974)
Mayberry R.F.D. (1968–1971)
The Brady Bunch (1969–1974)

MY THREE SONS (1960–1972)

My Three Sons ran on ABC and then CBS for a total of twelve years, and it features the life of widower and aeronautical engineer Steven Douglas (Fred MacMurray), his three sons, Chip (Stanley Livingston), Robbie (Don Grady), and Mike (Tim Considine), and their live-in maternal grandfather, Bub O'Casey (William Frawley and then William Demarest). *My Three Sons* represents a new trend in 1960s television—that of the all-male household and/or the household with the mother removed. Friedan recognizes this trend in the early 1960s, noting "the malevolence with which television eliminated mothers from the family circle: Does the new plethora of widowers, bachelor fathers, and unmarried mature men on television, who pay a maid or houseboy or, perhaps, a robot to get the household drudgery done, signify unconscious rebellion against that 'housewife' altogether?"[10] I find that these shows, rather than representing rebellion, are further proof of the variety and ambiguity so typical of 1960s television, as it sought to retain as many viewers as possible within an ever-changing social climate. *My Three Sons* is unique in that, even though a mother character is not present in the show, she is not replaced by a hired maid. Bub performs the duties typical of the mother character in similar shows, and that contributes to an interesting reading of the function of housework.

   The cast experienced changes over the years, as is typical when a show is as long running as *My Three Sons*, so this analysis focuses on the early episodes before William Frawley left the show. Immediately in the series, housework is used to identify Bub as the "housekeeper" in the family, and for

this reason, most of this analysis focuses on his character. First, Bub is signified iconographically as the "housekeeper" of the family because he wears a
towel tucked into the front of his pants. This serves as a masculinized version
of the more feminine apron, but Bub's character is feminized in other ways
through his interactions with the boys, as he performs feminized activities
such as teaching them to dance and serving them tea. This is a trend we will
see implemented more obviously in subsequent decades with *Mr. Belvedere*
and *Golden Girls*. Viewing Bub's work as maternal practice is important, as
it removes the biological elements of mothering activities. Through this lens,
Bub is simply willing to recognize the vulnerability of a family in need and
meet those demands through housekeeping activities. This perspective is also
useful when understanding the characters Aunt Bee (*The Andy Griffith Show*)
and Hazel (*Hazel*) later in this decade, and in a multitude of shows featuring
housekeepers in the 1980s. These housekeeper characters embody the notion
that biology does not necessarily matter when deciding to engage in maternal
practice, as Ruddick defines it.

Regarding housekeeping, Bub performs most of the housework, aside
from washing and drying dishes, which is often shared by Steven and the
children. These moments are used to depict Steven's emotional connection to
his boys, as they often discuss important topics over dishes, such as girls and
their classes. Housework provides the opportunities for emotional connection between family members, and the children seek father's advice in these
moments of service and mutual effort.

Even though William Frawley's gruff acting style works to counteract the
feminization of his character, it still occurs through housework and dialogue.
In the episode, "Chip Off the Old Block," a makeup salesman knocks on
the door, asking for the lady of the house. Chip immediately calls for Bub,
revealing him as "the lady of the house." Bub goes to the door and tells the
salesman he is the "closest thing to a lady in this house." Housework is used
to inject a jealous and emotional aspect to Bub's character—traits that are
often signified by visual culture as feminine traits. Bub cooks the meals,
tells the boys to wash their hands, but when Steven is unable to eat the meal
he prepared, Bub gets upset, even though the food will still be consumed
by the sons. As in other shows, Bub's housework represents his desire to
preserve and meet the demands of family. This is evidenced by his emotion
over family members not accepting his service. The service fulfills him, just
as it does female characters of similar roles in other shows. Later, Bub gets
jealous when Steven prefers the cooking of his new lady friend over Bub's
meals. Similar to the patterns of housework in *The Goldberg's*, Bub uses
his housework to compete for affection, but I do not regard this negatively.
I believe it is another example of the deeply fulfilling qualities of service,
and when housework is viewed as maternal practice—the act of preserving

life—performers of housework want to know others are benefitting from these preservative efforts.

It is interesting that we rarely see Bub experience leisure, as we did with many of the housewife characters of the 1950s. When Bub is unable to perform certain scheduled tasks, like cooking dinner or washing dishes because the water isn't working in the house, for example, rather than take a break to wait for the water to be turned back on, Bub will perform additional, often superfluous, housework, like polishing the bannister. Ultimately, it seems the show seeks to exaggerate Bub's "housewife" qualities, potentially for comedic effect, and he consequently appears to do more housework than other similar characters of the era. Still, in general, Bub's service to his family through housekeeping is endearing and the inherent love is clear.

One important thing to note about Bub, though, is he is perhaps the only housekeeping character until the 1980s to set explicitly his own housekeeping limits. When the boys ask for too much, Bub will tell them he is willing to do only so much. For example, in the episode "Chip Off the Old Block," Mike is asking Bub for a missing sock. Bub replies, "I only wash the socks; I don't ball them." Female performers of housework never identify such boundaries, until perhaps *Mama's Family* and *Gimme A Break!* in the 1980s. Television uses dialogue such as this to suggest that housework is not as natural for males as it is for females. Bub is only willing to do so much—he will clean the clothes, but he's not going to fold them—whereas the sacrifices of televised women performing housework know no bounds. Bub's dialogue seems determined to masculinize him and perhaps combat a characterization that regularly functions as "the lady of the house." That said, if we are to analyze Bub's housework, even with his self-established boundaries, as maternal practice, we see the same qualities of preservation revealed in his work.

THE ANDY GRIFFITH SHOW (1960–1968)

The Andy Griffith Show ran for eight years on CBS, and starred Andy Griffith as widowed sheriff Andy Taylor of the town of Mayberry, Don Knotts as deputy Barney Fife, Frances Bavier as Andy's Aunt Bee, and Ron Howard as Andy's son Opie. This show serves as another example of a series featuring a widower and an absent mother, but in this show, duties typical to the mother character are assumed by Aunt Bee. Actually, the first episode centers on this issue, as prior to Aunt Bee, Opie and Andy had been cared for by their housekeeper Rose, to whom Opie was very attached. *The Andy Griffith Show* exemplifies a trend that begins in the 1960s and is furthered in the 1970s and 1980s—that of the "housekeeper" who does far more than housework, and becomes integrated into the family, filling the roles not just of an absent mother, but often of both parents. In the 1950s, only occasionally would housekeepers be present, and they would rarely, if ever, have significant roles on television. In the 1960s, we find multiple shows like *The Andy Griffith Show, Hazel,* and *Mayberry R.F.D.* where a woman who is not the mother, cares for the family as if she were the mother, cooking cleaning, parenting, and generally serving their emotional needs. For this reason, we also see these characters surprisingly claim a contentment and fulfillment in serving a family that is not necessarily their own. The same preservative love this study has highlighted with other representations of housework are certainly present with these characters as well, thus indicating these qualities—love, sacrifice, and strength—that I believe are inherent to housework activity are present whether the character is related or not.

In the episode "The New Housekeeper," Opie is against the idea of Aunt Bee moving in to care for Andy and him, as he claims Rose is the "best ever," and "nobody is like Rose." He decides he would rather have no housekeeper than a new housekeeper like Aunt Bee. The morning she is to arrive, Opie attempts to set the table and make breakfast himself. The scene makes it clear Opie does not know what he doing. When he drops a grapefruit, he cleans it off using the floor-cleaning brush; he burns the toast; and the eggs have been cooking on the stove for forty-five minutes. Andy enters and comments sarcastically about the fine job Opie did. Opie says, "See Pa, this shows we don't need Aunt Bee. Can't we just tell her to turn around and go back?" This is significant because housework is used to signify the need for a woman in the house. Contrary to Opie's dialogue, he and Andy clearly *do* need Aunt Bee, and the need for a female in this all-male household is established upfront in the series.

Interestingly, it is also established in the first episode that Aunt Bee needs them as well. When she arrives to the house, Andy thanks her for coming, and she in turn thanks him, saying, "All those young'uns I raised are all grown now, so when you called . . . well, that's why I got on my knees and thanked heaven I had a place to go and something to do." Unfortunately, Aunt Bee's dialogue here, in addition to subsequent episodes, reinforces the stereotype of women being more "naturally suited" than men for housekeeping and parenting, as Hesse-Biber and Carter claim that "housework has come to be equated with what women are, not what they do" and that some believe "women have an innate talent for housework, enjoy it more, or have a greater need for clean clothes, household order, and balanced meals."[11] Aunt Bee's dialogue certainly contributes to this notion, but just as I have argued previously, it is not that she enjoys the housework specifically, but rather that she is fulfilled through the satisfaction of meeting the preservative needs of others, of contributing on any level to the preservation of life in general. I believe her character's housekeeping signifies—and viewers recognize—strength in these aspects of the televised housework.

Aunt Bee's "need" to care for someone frequently underpins the plots of the aforementioned and subsequent episodes. Opie reveals that the reason he does not want Aunt Bee to replace Rose is that she can't play baseball, fish, or catch frogs with him—activities that are often gendered male by visual culture, but which many housekeeper characters take on, in addition to the more feminine activities. (In the show *Hazel*, for example, Hazel teaches Harold how to play football.) Aunt Bee tries to learn these activities to please Opie, but she is not successful. She decides to leave the family, but at the end of the episode, as she is getting into the car, Opie comes running out of the house yelling that he wants her to stay because *she* needs *him*—she needs him to teach her all of the things she can't do. Whereas Opie is talking about fishing and catching frogs—activities she does not actually need to learn—viewers likely connected with the actual message of this scene: Aunt Bee's character *does* need them, as caretaking—preserving life—equals fulfillment, self-worth, and purpose for her, and this is signified through her housework.

These issues are present in subsequent episodes, as well. For example, in the episode "Andy and Opie, Housekeepers," Aunt Bee is chiding them for being so messy. Her arms are full of laundry and dishes, when she mentions that she will be leaving for a few days and they will need to take care of themselves. As Aunt Bee prepares to leave, her dialogue reflects clear concern that the males will not be able to take care of themselves, even though they assure her they can. As she leaves, Opie says, "Boy, she sure does go on, doesn't she?" Andy responds, "That's because she loves us, Opie, and she worries about us, wants us to be healthy and well taken care of." This is significant because it suggests that the male characters understand Aunt Bee does not do housework because she is "naturally suited" for it or because she has an innate ability, but perhaps because she is naturally suited, just as they are, for the practice of preserving life. Andy indicates that she does it because it is a way for her to show love, to sacrifice for others, to find fulfillment in servitude. Incidentally, in the end, Andy and Opie avoid the housework all week, live in a mess, and then begrudgingly make a mad dash to clean the day she arrives. (At one point, Opie breaks a dish, and Andy isn't mad about the broken dish, but rather he is frustrated that he had just taken the time to clean the broken dish, indicating his complete disdain for housework—a quality we don't often see in female characters of the era.) After they finish cleaning, they realize their ability to clean will make Aunt Bee feel unneeded, so they mess up the house again. In this way, Aunt Bee *needs housework to feel needed*, so housekeeping activities again signify connection to the things in life that matter to her character. At the same time, this episode proves that

Andy and Opie are capable of being responsible for their own housework, and television reveals through other shows that if Andy and Opie were females, they would be responsible for this work. Aunt Bee's character exists so that the males do not *have* to do the housework. Still, Aunt Bee's fulfillment through seeing Andy and Opie benefit from her labor remains a sign of feminine strength.

It is interesting, I believe, to note one minor part of this show. When Aunt Bee leaves, as she does in this episode, and Andy needs to go to work, Opie, who is only six years old, is left alone all day in the house. This indicates that Andy's "need" for Aunt Bee is not necessarily for child-care—that perhaps her only function from his perspective is to cook and clean. We see her care for Opie in almost all episodes—care that is similar to that of a mother—but the implication in the scenes where Opie stays home alone with no supervision is that the perception of Aunt Bee *actually* being needed for child-rearing in addition to housework, may be her perception alone. It also makes her statements like, "What would you do without me?" seem foolish, as viewers have just witnessed that Andy and Opie are perfectly capable of cooking and cleaning on their own. In this sense, Aunt Bee's character is made a fool and the impact of her preservative love is diminished. Even though Aunt Bee's character exists to serve them, the show implies that Andy and Opie need Aunt Bee less than she needs them. In a way, this strengthens my argument. I find that housework significations are less significant when television depicts them as not *actually* being needed to preserve life. Even if we, the viewers, know how unnecessary Aunt Bee is, but she does not know it, her housekeeping activities take on a foolish quality, as the show suggests the males are, in reality, giving more to Aunt Bee than she is giving to them, even though she is living a life in service to them. This does not change the love and sacrifice inherent in her work, but it, like June Cleaver's childish questions about parenting in the 1950s, does unfortunately reinforce a depiction of women as passive dupes of patriarchy.

HAZEL (1961–1966)

Hazel aired for five years on NBC and then CBS, and it depicts the life of live-in maid Hazel Burke (Shirley Booth), and the Baxter family, George (Don DeFore), Dorothy (Whitney Blake), and their son Harold (Bobby Buntrock). Like Aunt Bee on *The Andy Griffith Show*, Hazel is not the mother of the family, yet she runs the house and also does most of the child-rearing. However, unlike Aunt Bee's character, Hazel is in charge of this household. In fact, much of the comedy occurs through her strong personality, boldness, and total management of the home. Incidentally, this show is one of few earlier programs with a female cowriter, which may contribute to Hazel's characterization. Regardless, her character is integrated completely into the family—she is one of them. Even the iconography of the show intro indicates this, when the Baxters are eating breakfast and Hazel pushes her way onto the seat next to them, forcing them to make room for her both on the bench and in the family.

Housework is significant in this series for several reasons. Hazel uses housework to ignore dialogue, mainly from patriarch George, that she does not want to hear. She will sing while she serves him coffee and he will ask her to stop so he can work, for example. Hazel continues to sing and serve as if he said nothing. When he is chiding her for something, she will often continue cooking and ask him "does this need more salt" in the middle of his lecture. Housework functions as a way for Hazel to ignore and appear distracted from issues she does not want to hear or address. Considering George is her employer and the supposed patriarch, it is often quite humorous to see Hazel appear unaffected by his actions and lectures. She prioritizes her housework in a way that tempers her potentially discourteous actions, which consequently makes her appear humorous instead of disrespectful. It is the loving and sacrificial qualities that enable housework to function in this way, as Hazel's ignoring George might seem rude if she weren't simultaneously performing an activity that is in service to him. Hazel's potential insolence is balanced by her dutiful service.

Similarly, like *I Love Lucy*, Hazel often uses housework to manipulate. In the episode, "Hazel Makes a Will," when she learns George has just secured a big new account, she decides she is due for a raise. She begins to use her housework as manipulation, trying to convince George to consider her raise. She offers to make him h'ordeurves and cooks his favorite dessert, for example. When she asks George to fix a broken brick on the porch, he refuses, claiming he doesn't have supplies. It is important to note that George performs almost no household duties, even when they are requested of him. He always claims he needs to work, thus reinforcing common images of the day, where "women were shown as naturally suited for housework and men for employment."[12] George's constant insistence that he cannot play football with his son, cannot enjoy the company of his wife, and cannot fix things around the house because he must work contributes to the strict oppositional construct represented in visual culture of the era—women should perform certain tasks and men others. But with regard to George fixing the brick specifically, Hazel ends up falling on the loose brick, and she is able to use George's lack of housework as manipulation as well.

Hazel's most significant contribution to this study, however, is that it is a unique example of a housekeeper also assuming the duties of both mother and father to the children, more so than the parent characters themselves. This show is possibly the most egregious example of uninvolved parents, especially with the mother character Dorothy. Even though Leibman is referencing shows of the 1950s, her assessment is consistent with the show *Hazel* when she states that "television programs minimize a mother's importance more discretely, either by manipulating the mother to be party to her own self-effacement or by structuring the narrative so that she only hangs about the periphery."[13] Dorothy's lack of involvement in her family is so egregious, she often has entire episodes with only a handful of lines. Duties that would normally be performed by mother and father are often handled exclusively by Hazel. For example, when Harold wants to learn to play football, George doesn't have time, so Hazel gladly teaches him. Even when the football gets stuck in the neighbor's chimney, Hazel gets a ladder and retrieves it herself from the roof—a task that television would certainly gender as being male in most cases. Hazel notices Harold's dirty hands and tells him to wash up for dinner, even when his parents are standing right next to him. In the evening scenes, when George is seated on the couch reading the newspaper—a scene typical to many shows of the 1950s and 1960s—even though other visual texts often present mother sewing or reading a book, Dorothy is usually seated next to him doing absolutely nothing. Furthermore, when George is working in his study, she will often approach him about spending time with her. He will apologize that she is bored, but claim he has to work. Interestingly, these are the same moments where Hazel is either teaching Harold to play football, reading a book to him, or playing checkers with him. (In fact, even when Hazel is bed-ridden, she will still spend time playing checkers on her bed with Harold.)

In other words, Hazel is enjoying activities with Dorothy's son, while Dorothy is claiming boredom to George. Dorothy's character could choose time with her son over boredom, but she views this as "Hazel's job." Even after situations where the show has presented Hazel as playing with Harold all day, versus the parents, following dinner, the parents will get ready to go to a friend's house to play bridge. My point here is not to disparage Dorothy's characters, but to make a greater point regarding housework's connection to fulfillment. Hazel performs almost all of the housework and child-rearing in the Baxter household, while Dorothy is often depicted as bored (even to the extent that her dialogue reflects this). Dorothy really is the passive mother character Leibman describes, who is "not depicted as being important for the emotional needs of [her family]."[14] However, Leibman's further claim that "it is her very culinary duties that cause mother's familial exclusion," that "during the ubiquitous dinner and breakfast scenes, the women are usually up and about serving, rather than sitting at the table,"[15] ironically involves all of Hazel's duties, rather than Dorothy's. Yet, Hazel's performance of these tasks results in an outcome opposite to Leibman's description of similar characters of the 1950s. Hazel is clearly the happiest and most fulfilled character in the show.

Hazel's housework makes her not only the active center of the home, but often makes the very act of serving the focus of a scene. For example, Hazel often stands at the table next to the family while they eat, not just to serve them, but to engage them in conversation throughout the meal.

Through these housekeeping duties, Hazel is portrayed as the happiest, most active, most important, and most fulfilled character in the show. As Douglas says with regard to Samantha Stephens on *Bewitched*, Hazel "skillfully manage[s] the contradictions of being [both superior and subordinate],"[16] as she is subordinate in her role as servant, yet superior in her role as house manager. She navigates these contradictions through her housework. Her character exemplifies this study's claims that housework functions as a signifier of preservative love and feminine strength, and as viewers make meaning of this, as Hall puts it, connections between these duties and fulfillment are likely solidified.

Figure 3.1 *Hazel, Season One,* **"Hazel Makes a Will,"** © CPT Holdings, Inc., Courtesy Sony Pictures Television.

THE DICK VAN DYKE SHOW (1961–1966)

The Dick Van Dyke Show ran for five years on CBS and portrayed the work and home life of television-writer Rob Petrie (Dick Van Dyke), housewife Laura (Mary Tyler Moore), and son Richie (Larry Mathews). Laura performs the majority of household duties, but this show is significant in how the housework reinforces notions of women being "naturally suited" for it and enjoying the activity more than men. As with other shows, like *I Love Lucy* and *Hazel*, Laura uses housework to negotiate. In "The Sick Boy and the Sitter," where Rob wants to go out to a party but Laura feels they should stay home with Richie, they go back and forth in their argument by tossing liver in and out of a pan on the stove. The liver—the activity of cooking—functions as the substance of the argument, with its placement in or out of the pan indicating the winner of the disagreement. During this scene, Laura says, "Darling, I'm a woman and if I leave the house feeling the way I do, something will happen. It's called women's intuition." Rob responds by bargaining, "If you go, I'll go to two decorator shows and three PTA meetings." She acquiesces by saying, "Five PTA meetings and okay." What is being traded is unequal. Rob is trading something he wants to do—a dinner with friends and colleagues—while Laura is trading things she likely does not *want* to do, but *must* do out of love and a desire to preserve—PTA meetings. It underscores the notion that women have no interests outside of their family and home. While I believe characters such as Laura represent a type of fulfillment and strength that are born from serving and meeting the preservative demands of others, I argue against representations that suggest women have no interests of their own similar to those of their husbands. Still, the function of housework as a tool of negotiation and the mediator of disagreements is interesting. Incidentally, one particularly enjoyable aspect about the housework in this show is how Rob will use moments when Laura is cooking and cleaning to show her physical affection. This presents a dynamic where love is being exchanged between partners, one through loving servitude, the other through physical affection.

THE BEVERLY HILLBILLIES (1962–1971)

The Beverly Hillbillies aired on CBS for nine years and featured a country family who strikes oil and moves to Beverly Hills, California. The show depicts the Clampett family, widower Jed Clampett (Buddy Ebsen), his mother-in-law "Granny" Moses (Irene Ryan), daughter Elly May (Donna Douglas), and Jethro (Max Baer, Jr.) the son of Jed's cousin. This show represents one of the first examples of what Marc called deeply escapist television in this decade, where "despite the commercial success of *The Dick Van*

Dyke Show, it inspired no spin-offs or even any obvious imitators. Instead, shows such as Paul Henning's *The Beverly Hillbillies* and William Asher's *Bewitched* (and their spin-offs and imitators) came to dominate the sitcom through the 1960s."[17] In this series, housework is often used to convey the family's ignorance. For example, in the episode "The Clampetts Meet the Dodgers," Jed is invited to play golf, but since players use terms like "birdies" and "eagles" to describe the sport, Jed thinks golfing is hunting. Granny, who is cooking most of the time, asks them to bring home some greens from their "hunt" for her to cook. In the end, they end up bringing home grass from the course and golf balls, and Granny cooks it all into a soup, using a golf club to stir the golf ball/golf course soup. Later, when Jethro is told he is going to play baseball because they need "big strong pitchers," Granny fetches a very large pitcher for them from her cabinet. Housework serves as a signifier of the family's ignorance and naiveté, especially regarding social norms in their new high-class, wealthy environment.

This is not portrayed negatively, though. Rather, the housework mistakes are endearing and comedic, for they represent the family's earnest efforts to survive and integrate, just as a family seeks integration with each other and their surroundings—efforts that symbolize devotion and dedication. This desire for integration is signified specifically through housework, and this aspect of the show contributes significantly to the study. As the family has altered their lifestyle, location, and social status, the ways in which they define preservation have also changed. These new rules for preservation are exposed primarily through Granny's activities of cooking and cleaning, and the family members discover new ways to function effectively—and to preserve life—in an unfamiliar situation through their activities of housework.

THE LUCY SHOW (1962–1968)

The Lucy Show ran on CBS for six years and served as a follow-up show to *I Love Lucy*. It involved a unique premise, where Lucille Ball stars as widow Lucy Carmichael and lives with her divorced friend, Vivian Bagley (Vivian Vance). They also live with Lucy's two children, daughter Chris (Candy Moore) and son Jerry (Jimmy Garrett), and Vivian's son Sherman (Ralph Hart). They all share a home in New York. This show is interesting on several levels. First, the animated intro presents Lucy and Vivian hammering the letters of the title up on the wall—an activity that would normally be considered masculine in nature. This animation indicates upfront that viewers can expect these female characters to function differently than in previous shows—to cover duties performed previously through mutual efforts of both fathers and mothers. The depiction of women hammering is used to indicate the absence of men, so housework serves as a mechanism, even through animation, to establish the basic premise of the show—two women running a household of five.

In this shared household, everyone contributes to the housework. There are no clearly defined roles. In fact, this is made explicit through dialogue. Lucy often asks everyone to pitch in and clean dishes after dinner so they can watch television together. The kids prepare their own breakfasts, and often, the boys clear the table so that Chris can have a chance to speak privately with her mother. Also, if Lucy is preparing food in the kitchen, Chris comes in and serves herself food, with Vivian entering to help as well. The show in general provides a unique model for "family" and consequently develops a distinctive depiction of housework—one that is explicitly shared. Interestingly, in order to make this living arrangement work, characters have learned to coexist, and much of this is the result of the shared treatment of housework. However, one point is worth mentioning. Even though this household is not all female, the two heads of the household are female, so it is worth comparing it to the show *My Three Sons* from the same decade—a show that reflects multiple male heads of household. When the family is all male, as it is in *My Three Sons*, gender-specific roles and duties are clearly established, with the female role going to the oldest and perhaps weakest member of the family, Bub. However, with two females running the household, gender-specific roles are not established and duties are shared among male, female, old, and young alike. I believe this reflects a strength and determination to preserve in female characters—traits that are reflected in their housework—that perhaps are not present in many male characters, as it takes strength, compromise, humility, and often sacrifice for unrelated individuals to integrate and coexist peacefully in a house when no explicit roles are established.

It is also worth noting that when female characters such as Lucy and Vivian in this show lose husbands, either to death or divorce, no one comes to their rescue to handle the domestic affairs. The show does not develop of character like Aunt Bee or Bub to move in and assume all of the housekeeping duties. The female characters, when placed in situation similar to single male characters, must pull double duty, working all day to earn a wage and then in the evenings to preserve the lives of their families. This reflects a significant female strength, as visual culture depicts women as having the ability to find logical solutions for survival in difficult situations and extraordinary strength to implement effective solutions. Visual culture of this era never depicts the solution for divorced or widowed women as housekeepers, but rather a shared-domestic-realm approach to household management, thus underscoring the resourcefulness of these female characters.

THE JETSONS (1962–1963)

The Jetsons is an animated sitcom that ran for a year on ABC and depicted the characters George and Jane Jetson, their children, Judy and Elroy, dog Astro, and older-model humanoid robot maid, Rosie. The intro of *The Jetsons* differs from previous sitcom intros, especially those of 1950s sitcoms like *The Donna Reed Show* and *Leave It to Beaver*, in a significant way, as it depicts a husband, instead of the wife, sending his family off to begin their days. In many shows of the 1950s and early 1960s, the intro depicts the mother character sending her children and husband off with a kiss through the front door, establishing her dominance in the domestic sphere. In *The Jetsons*, George flies his space car and, one by one, drops off all family members at their respective destinations for the day, indicating a unique focus on the public sphere in addition to the private. Housewife Jane is being dropped off at the mall to shop, and the implication that her schedule outside of the home is "busy" contributes to establishing the need to hire Rosie.

The character Rosie is hired as the Jetsons' robotic maid, and she performs almost all housework and some parenting, which typically contributes little to the plot. However, in a *Jetsons* special feature titled "Rosie the Robotic Maid," housework and housewife discontentment—issues that were central to feminist discourses of the era, especially after the release of Friedan's work in 1963—are addressed. The special feature opens with images of *The Flintstones*, and the voiceover says, "Since the dawn of time, housewives have struggled with the exhausting and mundane chores of housework." Jane then says, "Housework! Nothing but housework," and the narrator continues to describe how housework was interfering with Jane's time to go to the salon, go shopping, and gossip, finally asking, "What modern-day woman has the time?" Rosie is regarded as the "cure" for housework because she makes housework "a breeze." The remaining dialogue is as follows: The narrator asks, "Is Jane Jetson overwhelmed with domestic duties?" Jane responds, "It's just that housework gets me down." The narrator continues, "No, sir, Rosie cooks, cleans, and still finds time to play ball with Elroy. Yes, this aluminum-encased, battery-powered, robotic woman is the perfect answer for any modern family." (It is interesting that an inhuman robot would still be given the gender identity of "robotic woman," complete with ruffled apron and hat.) The message of this special feature seems to claim, in a tongue-in-cheek way, that the activity of housework is robotic in nature, does not require human qualities to be performed, and thus, can, and perhaps should, be accomplished by a machine. However, Rosie, a machine, is anything but inhuman, and this is revealed through her housekeeping and childcare. Even though Rosie isn't programmed to love, she actually displays the human qualities of love and concern through her housekeeping duties, especially in how she cares for the children. Therefore, through Rosie, *The Jetsons* reveals housework activity brings to the fore the inherent *human* attributes of preservative love, even when the character is anything but human.

THE PATTY DUKE SHOW (1963–1966)

The Patty Duke Show ran on ABC for three years and starred Patty Duke in both roles of identical cousins, Patty and Cathy Lane, who, despite looking alike, are very different in personality and interests. Additionally, the show included the mother and father characters of Martin Lane (William Schallert) and Natalie Lane (Jean Byron). Patty and Cathy perform a surprising amount of housework as teenagers, often washing dishes and preparing their own meals. However, one episode involves a treatment of housework worth mentioning, as it was released in September of 1963 and could be viewed as a direct response to parts of Friedan's *The Feminine Mystique*, released in February of that same year. In the episode "The Genius," Cathy is doing the dishes, when her aunt asks, "Didn't you do the dishes last night and the night before?" Cathy tells her that she and Patty regularly flip a coin to decide who will do the dishes that evening, and Patty is very lucky. Mother reprimands Patty for using a double-sided coin to ensure she doesn't have to do housework, and Patty claims she is treated as slave labor with all the housework she has to do. Later, Patty is in the kitchen doing dishes when her teacher visits the house to tell her parents she scored in the "genius" category on her intelligence test at school. The teacher says, "It is tragic that she is doing dishes because time spent doing dishes is time wasted that she could spend discovering a new vaccine." He continues, "Just imagine the mathematical formulas lost while she was doing the dishes!" The parents tell her they have decided she won't ever have to do dishes again, and the mother begins serving Patty breakfast in bed. (Incidentally, while most of Patty's and Cathy's housework is visible, the mother's housework is invisible. She is seen delivering breakfast to Patty, for example, but not preparing breakfast.) Later, it is revealed that Patty tricked the IQ test at school, and the punishment given to her by her parents involves performing an extensive amount of housework, as Mother tells her to do the dishes, clean her room, clean the hall closet and bathrooms, and iron.

This treatment of housework seems to be a direct response to some of the claims made by Friedan regarding housework and education. She argues that the more a woman's "intelligence exceeds [her] job requirements, the greater [her] boredom,"[18] and that the outcome of this boredom is unsurprising, when, according to Friedan, the reality remains that many women were using their sixteen years of education to perform the most menial of tasks—tasks that in the labor force would receive the lowest wages. The implication is that this education is wasted on these menial tasks, and the dialogue from this episode reflects this claim explicitly. The teacher actually equates the time Patty spends on housework with potentially lost medical, scientific, or mathematical discoveries. In this episode, housework signifies wasted time, wasted education, and functions as a form of punishment. When visual texts signify housework in this way, it is stripped of its endearing qualities. As I've mentioned before, it is not the task itself that I claim is fulfilling, but rather the understanding that someone benefits from the task and the acknowledgment of the love that is communicated through the task. These visual texts serve as vehicles for housework to function as this tool of loving communication. This communication can be two way as well, as children often understand housework on this level just as their parents do. However, in *The Patty Duke Show*, housework is often separated from its fulfilling qualities, rendered as merely a task that will earn the children privileges and not a form of communication, and consequently, functions as a signifier of punishment and wasted time—an outcome that likely has some connection to Friedan's claims earlier that year. This could be a result of the invisibility of mother's work. *The Patty Duke Show* depicts housework from the teenage perspective of Cathy and Patty—a perspective that regards domestic tasks as chores rather than the preservative activities of maternal practice.

PETTICOAT JUNCTION (1963–1970)

Petticoat Junction aired for seven years on CBS. The show is set outside of Hooterville, which would later become the setting for *Green Acres*, and depicts the activities of The Shady Rest Hotel. Characters include hotel owner Kate Bradley (Bea Benaderet), her uncle Joe Carson (Edgar Buchanan), and her three daughters Betty Jo (Linda Henning), Bobby Jo (Laurie Saunders), and Billie Jo (Meredith MacRae). Kate and her three girls perform housework for the guests of the hotel, which are mainly men. As owner of the hotel, Kate is a businesswoman. It is interesting how housework contributes to her characterization, as it is the first time we see cooked food being treated as actual currency—a function that both underscores her role in business and blurs public/private spheres. Kate pays for things with her cooking, as she will purchase train fares, for example, with chicken dinners and apple pies. Even though previous characters have used housework to manipulate and get what they want (e.g., Lucy in *I Love Lucy* and Hazel in *Hazel*), this treatment is different, as more of a business model is applied to the activity and function of housework.

It is no coincidence that this treatment of housework exists within a show where the lead character is a business-minded matriarch. Housewife characters of the 1950s and 1960s also perform their housework manageri-ally, in the same way a career woman might run her office. This depiction further convinced 1950s housewives struggling with the real-life drudgery of housework that, as Leibman puts it, this type of housewife "was a career woman after all; it's just that her career was the home and family."[19] But *Petticoat Junction* takes this a step further. Kate runs her hotel much like housewife characters are depicted running their households. She and the girls put a lot of love and care into their housekeeping, as they perform extra, unrequired duties for guests, such as picking fresh flowers to include with meals and taking special care not to awaken anyone while delivering meals.

Kate's treatment of her guests is very similar to a mother's treatment of her family in other shows. However, whereas these housewife characters don't necessarily receive anything tangible for their housework, Kate, the career-minded businesswomen, has figured out a way to use her resources cheaply and effectively and to receive tangible goods in exchange for her work. Her housework then is essentially waged work, which changes its signification, yet some of the same love and sacrifice seen in previous depic-tions of housework are still present here. In this way, *Petticoat Junction* presents a dichotomy. Kate and her daughters serve mainly men, so the show maintains the strict oppositional construct that implies that men are suited for employment and women are suited for caretaking. At the same time, Kate's housework is paid a wage, so her character is interestingly presented as one that exists simultaneously in both spheres of male/public/employment and female/private/housekeeping. Consequently, the preservative qualities brought to the fore in this study change significantly in *Petticoat Junction*. Kate is still engaging in preservative love, but because her housework must be maintained for her business to flourish, she is preserving life in a more indirect way. In other housekeeping models within domestic sitcoms, mothers have engaged in a maternal practice that directly sustains life through food and care. Kate preserves life through housekeeping by making a wage that keeps her girls fed and healthy, so while the model changes, the desire to meet the demands of children and the strength inherent to that commitment remains the same.

GILLIGAN'S ISLAND (1964–1967)

Gilligan's Island aired for three years on CBS and starred Bob Denver as Gilligan, Alan Hale, Jr. as The Skipper, Jim Backus as millionaire Thurston Howell III, Natalie Schafer as Eunice Howell, Tina Louise as movie star Ginger Grant, Russell Johnson as Professor Roy Hinkley, and Dawn Wells as Mary Ann Summers. The premise involves a group of people who took a "three-hour tour" aboard the SS *Minnow* in Honolulu. The ship is caught in a storm and the characters end up stranded on an island. As they collectively make a home on the island, tasks are generally shared between genders. The Skipper cooks breakfast, Gilligan does the laundry, Mary Ann and Ginger fish and prepare dinner.

As the series progresses, however, these tasks become more gender-specific, with Mary Ann and Ginger performing the cooking and laundry duties, while the men build huts and think of ways to get off the island—tasks that, unfortunately, reinforce notions that males are more suited for work requiring logic and females for work requiring feeling or care. However, one episode addresses directly the issue of the gender-specific roles the group has naturally created while on the island. In the episode "St. Gilligan and the Dragon," Mary Ann and Ginger are serving the men breakfast when they threaten to go on strike if the men don't fulfill their promise to build them a private female hut of their own. The men claim to have been too busy with other things, so the women remove their breakfast before the group finishes eating, claiming they will do no more housework until the men build their hut. The building of the hut is not ongoing labor. Once it is built, the labor ceases. So the women are willing to trade their ongoing labor of daily cooking and cleaning for the men's temporary labor—a trade that seems unbalanced at best—yet the men are still unwilling. The division of labor established by *Gilligan's Island* is consistent with Hesse-Biber and Carter's description of housework in reality:

> Not only is there a discrepancy in the number of hours of work done by men and women, there is also a qualitative difference in the kinds of domestic tasks they perform. Even within housework, there is such a thing as "women's work" and "men's work." Women are most likely to cook, wash dishes, do laundry, clean the house, and take care of children. On the other hand, men do most maintenance and repair work . . . women's work comprises mostly daily jobs and time-bound jobs. Men's jobs are time-flexible. . . . Thus, men have more discretion in the allocation and distribution of their time.[20]

With regard to gendered divisions in the aforementioned episode, Ginger states, "We think women should have the same rights as men." This is interesting considering their request of a hut for continuous housework service is already unequal. Still, the Professor responds, "You women are going to have to face the facts. Historically, it's the man who decides what should be done." This show highlights the importance of mutual efforts that underpinned 1950s household models in visual culture. Women were depicted as fulfilled in their servile roles because they recognized the significance of their work when it functioned to balance a system of mutual efforts to preserve the lives of family members. When the efforts become too one-sided, the scale is unbalanced, and one side becomes disgruntled—an issue that served as the substance of multiple plots in various shows. Visual culture in the 1950s and 1960s especially reinforced the importance of established roles and mutual efforts—an ideology we see underscored by *Gilligan's Island*.

The group divides by gender, with the girls establishing their own camp, claiming they have taken care of themselves before and can do it again. The rest of the episode involves scenes depicting their need for each other—their need to work together. (Incidentally, furthering the inequality already established by the "women's work" and "men's work" divisions, the episode presents the four dreams of the males—dreams that each involve unique storylines of women in complete servitude to them. No such dream sequence is granted to the women.) The women are shown to need the protection of the males, and the males fail at every attempt to cook or clean. The inconsistency of this portrayal is a frustrating aspect of the show, as the males have been seen in numerous prior episodes performing housework quite successfully. The Skipper cooks well, as he was employed as a cook before becoming a captain, and Gilligan performs laundry. However, in an attempt to further gendered housework activity, the episode depicts males and females as being incapable of crossing into each other's spheres—of performing tasks outside of what is deemed "women's work" or "men's work."

Most important, with regard to the main argument of this study, Gilligan admits at one point in the episode, "You know, without the women, cleaning clothes is kind of fun, and cleaning the hut is kind of enjoyable, and preparing the meals is kind of pleasant." Gilligan is not as committed to the gender dispute as the other male characters, and his dialogue reflects an appreciation for the fulfilling qualities of housework and general service to others—an appreciation for the strength inherent in committing to preservation and meeting the needs of others. Unfortunately, Gilligan is also depicted by the show as the buffoon in the group, who is easily duped by others and regularly feminized, by wearing an apron or even women's clothes while performing housework tasks such as laundry.

BEWITCHED (1964–1972)

Bewitched aired for eight years on ABC and starred Elizabeth Montgomery as housewife witch Samantha Stephens, Dick York and then Dick Sargent as her mortal husband Darrin, and Agnes Moorehead as Samantha's mother. In this show, Samantha longs to be what she considers a "normal housewife," and in marrying her mortal husband Darrin, she swears off her magical powers.

Figure 3.2 *Bewitched, Season One,* **"Be It Ever so Mortgaged,"** © CPT Holdings, Inc., Courtesy Sony Pictures Television.

If *Gilligan's Island* reinforced gendered divisions of labor, *Bewitched* took this issue even further. The show reminds viewers often that Samantha not only chooses these divisions, but is fulfilled by this arrangement and housewifery in general. In the episode "Fastest Gun on Madison Avenue," for example, Samantha tells Darrin, "You know there's a lot more to running a house than most people think." Darrin replies, "Honey, I think it's wonderful the way you've adjusted," and Samantha claims, "I love being a housewife." Darrin then asks, "Are you sure you won't get bored once the novelty has worn off?" Confidently, Samantha says, "How could I be bored being married to someone like you?" Dialogue such as this confirms and perhaps exaggerates her confidence in her decision, as well as acknowledges the fact that "housewife boredom," as Freidan notes and as I mentioned in the beginning of this chapter, had become a part of the national dialogue.

With regard to gender-specific roles in the show, Douglas claims that "While the show reaffirmed the primacy of traditional female roles and behaviors, it also provided powerful visual representations of what many young women would like to do if they just had a little power: zap that housework and a few men as well."[21] However, the premise of the show involves a witch who has the power to zap her housework, but chooses not to, and I argue this is because the character is depicted as one who recognizes and chooses the fulfillment inherent in preserving the lives of her family members.

Darrin almost never performs housework—an aspect of the show that is often difficult to watch in the twenty-first century. Prior to this show, as this analysis has shown, it is common to see the male help out with tasks such as dishes or setting the table. Darrin performs almost no household tasks, so the show adheres strictly to oppositional constructs where the male is employed and the female cares exclusively for the home. Regardless of intention or whether the show, with largely male writing teams, was responding directly to Friedan's claims about housewifery, this study is interested in how this visual text signified housework and how viewers made meaning in these texts. Even with all of Darrin's sexist dialogue, Samantha appears fulfilled. Her character seems genuinely happy to serve her family, without the assistance of magic because the magic would negate the act of service. Samantha attempts housework without magic, not necessarily because Darrin demands it, but because the magic strips her of the satisfaction she experiences in engaging in maternal practice—in meeting the demands of her family members. This aspect of her character likely serves as a form of validation for women in reality. Whether female viewers worked outside of the home or as housewives, the large majority handled the housekeeping duties of their homes almost exclusively in the 1960s. Samantha's character, while far from normal, likely validated the housework of 1960s women by emphasizing the love, the self-sacrifice, and the potential fulfillment of "women's work," instead of the drudgery. Samantha's commitment to her home represents a joy that I believe women share in reality when those they love benefit from their efforts. When we evaluate Samantha's housework as maternal practice instead of menial labor, her resistance to using magic can be understood as a housewife's resistance to hiring a housekeeper or nanny. Performing the tasks of maternal practice, of preserving life, loses its meaning and significance, in a way, when magic or housekeeper are used to buffer the challenges of housework, thus reinforcing the strength inherent in mother's commitment to this work. Samantha appears to understand this about the activities of maternal practice, and in all likelihood, mothers in reality understood it, as well.

THE MUNSTERS (1964–1966)

The Munsters aired for two years on CBS and starred Fred Gwynne as patriarch Herman Munster, Yvonne De Carlo as his wife Lily, Butch Patrick as their son Eddie, Al Lewis as Grandpa, and Beverly Owen and Pat Priest as niece Marilyn. This show depicts a family dynamic much like *The Donna Reed Show* and *Leave It to Beaver*—in fact, the intro follows the same model set forth by these 1950s shows of mother kissing her family goodbye as they leave for the day—but the characters are far from ordinary. The horrific elements of the show are often revealed through the characters' housework activities, which parallel much of what is seen in the 1950s. Like other televised housewives, Lily is always making and serving breakfast, but when she makes oatmeal, it is in a cauldron, for example, and when she serves Eddie, he eats while hidden in a cabinet, and when she asks Grandpa how he would like his eggs, he replies "Gloomy side up, please." Lily performs her housework just as Donna Stone, for example, but the humor is born in how ordinary they treat the extraordinary nature of their family. Her dialogue will often include statements, such as the line in "My Fair Munster," "How would you like to have to clean nine rooms and a dungeon every day?" When Lily offers food like "warm ladyfingers" to family or guests, she means actual lady fingers, and Herman will often garden, but his attention is focused on caring for the weeds instead of the plants or blooms. Their housework is "performed" in a way that reflects normalcy (and certainly normalcy to them), but parts of the activity also reflect the strange, the horrific, the abnormal—a juxtaposition that is quite comedic.

In fact, the "normal" aspects of the family's housework, I argue, are the loving, preservative qualities shared by most of the performers of housework discussed in this study. These qualities are inconsistent with viewers' preconceived notions of monsters, an aspect of the show that creates mirth. But Lily's and Herman's care for the emotional needs of their children, and of Grandpa, is clear in their housework, whether through Lily sewing a doll's ear back on for Eddie or through the family's patience with Grandpa when his experiments in the dungeon constantly make the electricity go off, rendering certain household tasks impossible. Their household duties signify the same sacrificial qualities they do in other shows within more "normal" televised families; thus the family unit in *The Munsters*, like *Bewitched*, signifies perhaps a redefinition for what constitutes "normal" or "natural," but maintains the inherent love and strength of housekeeping duties. Like *Bewitched*, *The Munsters* draws on the common 1960s trope to use the supernatural or the horrific to question what is normal or abnormal within the family dynamic, but this study finds that the preservative qualities of housework specifically provide a level of common ground among visual texts of varying content.

THE ADDAMS FAMILY (1964–1966)

The Addams Family ran on ABC for two years, and even though it is often considered to be very similar to *The Munsters*, *The Addams Family* enjoyed more popularity and higher ratings than its competitor on CBS. Based on the characters in Charles Addams' cartoons in *The New Yorker*, characters include wealthy and romantic patriarch Gomez Addams (John Astin), wife Morticia (Carolyn Jones), daughter Wednesday (Lisa Loring), son Pugsley (Ken Weatherwax), Uncle Fester (Jackie Coogan), and Grandmama (Marie Blake), in addition to servants Lurch (Ted Cassidy) and Thing (a hand). The treatment of housework in this show is similar to *The Munsters*, but with a bit more magic involved. For example, in the episode "Halloween with the Addams Family," Morticia makes punch for a party by performing spells over a cauldron. She pours ingredients from tubes and beakers, until the punch begins to sizzle, smoke, and explode. When she gardens, she feeds the plants hamburgers, and when she requests to smoke, she merely crosses her arms until smoke forms around her. At the same time, much of Morticia's housework is less magical and a bit more "normal." She teaches Lurch to iron properly by hand, and she hangs curtains manually for guests. Scenes such as this are comedic because Morticia expresses a desire to be liked by her female guests, hence the "normal activity" of hanging new curtains to prepare for guests, yet she thinks nothing of the "abnormal activity" of asking Gorgo the gorilla and Thing to serve the ladies tea. The honesty of Morticia's efforts, though, is endearing, and her housework thus signifies the same care and love, despite the often horrific nature of her methods.

With regard to Morticia's and Gomez's relationship specifically, I would like to highlight one point. As described earlier with Morticia's spells, her housework, and most often her cooking, is depicted very scientifically. When she performs spells, we often see her use scientific instruments such as test tubes and beakers. Typically in visual cultures of the era, males are associated with things involving logic and intelligence, and females with intuition and domesticity, and televised male characters are often astronauts (Tony Nelson in *I Dream of Jeannie*), doctors (Alex Stone in *The Donna Reed Show*), or architects (Mike Brady in *The Brady Bunch*), for example. However, Morticia's character is depicted as having an understanding of science—something that is revealed through her housework. I argue that it is no coincidence that *The Addams Family* also presents a married couple very much in love, one that is physically romantic in almost every episode. In fact, Gomez's attraction to Morticia is a major part of the show's premise. Morticia's character breaks the mold created by the visual cultures of the 1950s and 1960s by being both a loving housewife and a spell-performing scientist (in a way, she is similar to Kate's ability to exist simultaneously in both private and public spheres as a domestic businesswoman in *Petticoat Junction*), and Gomez's response of intense physical attraction signifies an interesting dynamic regarding male and female representation in this show. Morticia's "science" is integrated into her housework, making the "science" both a self-serving interest and a self-sacrificing activity. It is this integration,

I argue, that makes Morticia's character unique and contributes to Gomez's uncontrollable desire for her. The show signifies the idea that a woman who can exist successfully in both male and female spheres is perhaps the ideal woman—a signification that runs contrary to the analyses of 1950s housewifery, those upholding the idea that the ideal woman is one in complete servitude to her family.

Even with this assessment of Morticia, however, she remains surprisingly similar to other mother characters of her era, and this is revealed through her housekeeping activities. She is depicted as a happy housewife who regards her domestic work as integral to sustaining the lives of her family members. Through this lens, Morticia's maternal practice renders her unorthodox approaches to housework as lovingly normal.

GREEN ACRES (1965–1971)

Green Acres ran on CBS for six years and depicted married couple Oliver Wendell Douglas (Eddie Albert) and Lisa Douglas (Eva Gabor), who move from a penthouse apartment in New York city to a rural farm near the location of its sister show *Petticoat Junction*. Much of the sexism of this show is disturbing, even when meant to be comedic, but with regard to this study of housework, its contributions are significant. My claim thus far has been that housework signifies preservative love and a commitment to meet the demands of others, and those qualities, in turn, attach a level of strength to female characters that is often ignored in feminist analyses of television. I am arguing that the ability of these women to put the needs of others before their own is a sign a great strength, and that they are indeed fulfilled in both representation and reality through the satisfaction of preserving life and through seeing others benefit from these labors.

Lisa's character in *Green Acres* furthers my argument because she is depicted as being self-serving. She does relinquish her beloved New York apartment to fulfill the dreams of her husband—an act of self-sacrifice, indeed—but her character maintains her self-serving desires of vanity even within a new environment that requires her to develop qualities of self-sacrifice. Therefore, even though Lisa is portrayed as loving her husband, she lacks the commitment to preservation that other female characters embody, and is consequently ineffective in her housework activity. I argue that Lisa's character lacks the strength of self-sacrifice that is required for these duties to be fulfilling for these female characters, and her housework signifies this deficiency. In the episode, "Lisa's First Day on the Farm," Lisa explores her new house with concern, especially when Oliver tells her the kitchen is the most important room in a farmhouse and shows her how to use a stove.

The show establishes immediately that Lisa has likely not performed even the most basic of housekeeping tasks. In *Bewitched*, Samantha's character receives a similar treatment, as she is unfamiliar performing housework without magic—something she must do upon marrying Darrin. But the difference in these characters, and the reason Samantha transitions to "happy housewife" in a way Lisa does not, is a difference of desire. Samantha has a strong desire to serve Darrin because she is fulfilled by seeing him benefit from her efforts, while Lisa maintains a strong desire to serve herself, even if in addition to Oliver. I believe this aspect of her character makes effective housework impossible, and it is the reason she fails at most tasks. The message seems clear. Without preservative love, housework is ineffective.

This is often revealed through her dialogue. In the episode, "The Decorator," Lisa sleeps in, and Oliver responds by saying, "You'll feel better once you've had some breakfast." Lisa says, "Who's going to cook it? When I got married, I promised to love, honor, and obey. I didn't say anything about cooking." Later, Oliver wants her to take on more domestic responsibilities, claiming it is easy because she can just throw things in a pot. In this way, the character of Oliver is also responsible for stripping housework of its endearing qualities. I argue that when this occurs, housework signifies the menial tasks alone, not the relationship between task, love, self-sacrifice and fulfillment that more typical representations of housework signify.

A neighbor, Kate Bradley, from the show *Petticoat Junction*, comes over to teach Lisa how to cook, but even after instruction, Lisa fails, as her pancakes and coffee can't be tolerated by those she is serving. In the episode, "The Deputy," Oliver asks her for a shopping list so he can go to the store and get her what she needs for the house. She replies that she needs "nail polish remover, cold cream, and eye shadow." Oliver has to show her how to consider the needs of others when she makes a shopping list. And in the episodes "Double Drick" and "Culture," Lisa shows no concern for the value of her home when she throws away the dirty dishes she does not want to clean. These are examples of the ways in which *Green Acres* depicts housework as drudgery, and the ways the show, consequently, depicts Lisa as unfulfilled and restless. Unlike other shows, housework in *Green Acres* is removed from the preservative love and strength inherent in its activity, and even though it is often comedic, the housework then signifies something completely different—a menial, meaningless, unwaged, and unfulfilling task alone.

I DREAM OF JEANNIE (1965–1970)

I Dream of Jeannie aired for five years and starred Barbara Eden as Jeannie and Larry Hagman as astronaut Tony Nelson. On one of his missions, Tony discovers Jeannie's lantern on an island, and he becomes her "master," taking her home to live with him. Running concurrently with *Green Acres*, Lisa Douglas resists housework while Jeannie often wants to serve too much. Jeannie's desire to please Tony is frequently provides the comedy of the show. In the episode "Jeannie and the Kidnap Caper," Jeannie uses her magic to pour his coffee at breakfast, and he gets annoyed because he is trying to do it himself. She continues doing everything for him until he tells her to stop. In "How Lucky Can You Get," she is helping Tony pack, claiming, "I was just trying to be helpful." Tony stops here and says, "That's when I get into most of my trouble—when you're trying to be helpful." And in "How to be a Genie in Ten Easy Lessons," Jeannie pushes Tony to eat breakfast when he doesn't want to, and she not only makes food appear on the table immediately, it appears directly in his mouth as well.

Jeannie is overzealous in her housework because she is programmed to please her master in an inhuman way. In the first few seasons, her goal is to do this job well. Jeannie is completely the opposite of Lisa Douglas in *Green Acres*, as she is devoted to complete servitude of others, yet her housework often fails as well. Interestingly, Jeannie uses much more of her magic to

Figure 3.3 *I Dream of Jeannie, Season Two,* "How to be a Genie in Ten Easy Lessons," © CPT Holdings, Inc., Courtesy Sony Pictures Television.

perform housework in the earlier seasons than she does in the later seasons. This also coincides with Jeannie and Tony falling in love and getting married, and as Jeannie subsequently develops more human qualities, her service—her housework—changes as well. She, like Samantha Stephens, wants to perform more housework without magic because she grows to be fulfilled by these acts of preservative love. Similar to Lucy in *I Love Lucy*, Jeannie transitions from serving out of obligation to serving out of love, and this is signified directly through her housework activities. She attempts to cook without magic; she begins adhering to a budget rather than making things appear; and consequently, by the fifth season, she participates in a more egalitarian relationship with Tony. In an early episode, Tony declares, "I'm an astronaut, not a housekeeper," but in the fifth-season episode "Jeannie, the Matchmaker," Tony cleans the windows, saying, "I told Jeannie I'd help her around the house today." Housework evolves over this series from a signifier of obligation to one of preservation and fulfillment, and as the relationship between Tony and Jeannie changes to include mutual love and respect, housework evolves to embody the same qualities.

FAMILY AFFAIR (1966–1971)

Family Affair ran for five years on CBS and depicted the life of engineer and bachelor Bill Davis (Brian Keith), his butler Giles French (Sebastian Cabot), and his orphaned nieces and nephew Crissy (Kathy Garver) and twins Jody (Johnny Whitaker) and Buffy (Anissa Jones), whom he is attempting to rear. *Family Affair* adds another show to what Marc calls "a curious subgenre of domestic comedy . . . built around the principle of synthesizing suburban-esque Anderson-like family situations into urban bachelor households . . ."[22] Like *My Three Sons* and *The Andy Griffith Show*, this show is lacking a typical mother figure, although Bill is not a widower—he is a bachelor. He chooses to be single. Consequently, the home is a Manhattan apartment and the caretaker, or surrogate mother figure, is an English gentleman butler, Mr. French, who is the very picture of sophistication. He performs all of the housework and begrudgingly in the beginning, the child-rearing too. Whereas this study does not analyze extensively Mr. French's housework, it is important to include this show in the overall analysis because it introduces an interesting trend. When shows feature a single male living alone, as in *Family Affair* and later, *Diff'rent Strokes* and *Benson*, they have hired help perform the housework, as if television explicitly resists a male character who cleans his own home. However, when a show features one or multiple females living alone or together, as in *The Mary Tyler Moore Show*, *Rhoda*, *Laverne and Shirley*, and *Golden Girls*, they do their own housework without hired help.

Upon initial inspection, this fact about televised housework might lead to the conclusion that this is further reinforcement of gender stereotypes, where men are associated with logic and intelligence and women with intuition and domesticity, but the implications are deeper. From the perspective of housework as maternal practice, not as a desire merely to keep a clean house but a desire to preserve life, it would seem visual cultures regard females as desiring the preservation of life more strongly than male characters, and this is further indication of the feminine strength underscored in this study. These ideas will be explored later in many of these shows.

HERE'S LUCY (1968–1974)

Here's Lucy ran on CBS for six years and for a third time, starred Lucille Ball as Lucy Carter, a working single mother, and her two children Kim and Craig, who are played by Lucy's real-life children, Lucie Arnaz and Desi Arnaz, Jr. This show's contribution to representations of housework is significant, as it is one of the first examples not only of an open-floor-plan house, where we can view living room, kitchen, and backyard at once, but also of a messy house. The series opens this way, in fact, with an emphasis on the mess and Lucy's lack of time as a working mother to clean it alone. In the episode "Mod, Mod Lucy," Lucy enters the living room and begins picking up items and throwing them at the kids, telling them to get all of their stuff and take it to their bedrooms while she starts dinner. Lucy carries groceries into the kitchen and begins preparing a meal. Her kitchen is also messy, by television's standards. She has dishes in a rack out on the counter, for example. Even in the episode "Lucy Visits Jack Benny," when the family decides to take a vacation, their suitcases and the contents are strewed about the living room, making a complete mess, as they attempt to organize and get packed. The messiness of the entire house is explicit and signifies the family's lack of time for housekeeping duties. Through the messes and the open layout of the house, housework almost functions as its own character in this show. Lucy Carter is one of the first televised examples of a single woman who works to pay the bills and runs a household where she is the only adult inhabitant. For this reason, she makes housekeeping appear messy and frustrating. Still, her character chooses to cook meals instead of bringing them home and to clean messes instead of leaving them, thus indicating a commitment to the health and happiness of her children—a commitment to preservation that must fulfill her or she would not do it. Even within this framework, the "messy" and "frustrating" layers of housekeeping activity can be pulled back to reveal the love and self-sacrifice at the core of housework's signification.

Furthermore, *Here's Lucy* is another example of a professional single woman pulling double duty, while similar professional male characters of the era have housekeepers, aunts, or grandfathers who maintain the domestic sphere. Ultimately, this highlights Lucy's determination—her strength—in her willingness to recognize vulnerability and meet the demands of her children, even when that involves actively working in both private and public spheres.

MAYBERRY R.F.D. (1968–1971)

Mayberry R.F.D. aired on CBS for three years as a spin-off of *The Andy Griffith Show*. It depicts father and son, Sam (Ken Berry) and Mike Jones (Buddy Foster), with Aunt Bee (Frances Bavier) again playing the housekeeper to a different father-son duo. This show is established almost exactly as *The Andy Griffith Show*, where the supposed *need* for a housekeeper is revealed immediately. In the first episode, "Andy and Helen Get Married," Sam is frying hamburgers for dinner. He plates and serves the food for his son, while Mike enters with his coat, saying a button is missing. Sam tells him he will sew it on after dinner, so Mike begins eating. He grimaces immediately when he tries the food, claiming it has too much salt and he can't eat the potatoes. Sam responds that he "is doing the best [he] can," and Mike asks when they are going to get another housekeeper. As in *The Andy Griffith Show*, Aunt Bee moves in and recognizes immediately their dire need for her service. The house is dusty and she quickly gets to work, explaining that she can't wait to get acquainted with her kitchen, an experience which is shown explicitly to bring her great joy.

The next day, Aunt Bee gets to work, but her duties in this house involve fetching eggs from underneath chickens and milking cows—a situation that reflects some of the preindustrialization duties within the household, duties often performed by men and children, in addition to women. She no longer buys all of her supplies from the store. She struggles with this, as she is initially afraid of the animals. She eventually decides she does not have the courage to perform this type of housework and feels she must leave the home if she can't perform the housework properly. This is important because it signifies housework as courageous activity. This study has focused on the strength inherent in housework, but *Mayberry R.F.D.* takes this a step further and presents a framework where one must also be courageous in her housework in order to function successfully within it. When Aunt Bee can't find this courage, which she does eventually and stays, she is ashamed, as she ties her self-worth directly to her ability to meet the preservative demands of others. Her determination to perform housework properly and effectively is so strong, she eventually finds the courage—ready to "charge life in the raw"—to remain at the house, in their service.

THE BRADY BUNCH (1969–1974)

The Brady Bunch ran for five years on ABC and portrayed the marriage of two widowed individuals and the joining of their families. Characters include Mike Brady (Robert Reed), wife Carol (Florence Henderson), daughters Marcia (Maureen McCormick), Jan (Eve Plumb), and Cindy (Susan Olsen), and sons Greg (Barry Williams), Peter (Christopher Knight), and Bobby (Mike Lookinland), in addition to their fun-loving housekeeper, Alice Nelson (Ann B. Davis). The similarities between the show *Hazel* and *The Brady Bunch* are significant, as, like the character Hazel, Alice functions as the active center of the family, despite her supposed subordinate role. She is both subordinate, as a housekeeper, and superior, as everyone's source of sage advice, and she, too, navigates these contradictions through her housework. Alice's superior place in the family is established much like Hazel's—through the introduction. In *Hazel*, the introduction ends with the character forcing her way into the breakfast table to eat with the family, representing her place as an equal member of the family. This also happens in the end of *The Brady Bunch* intro, as the center square is reserved for Alice. This image signifies the centrality of the housekeeper, the one most responsible for meeting the demands of others, within the family structure.

Quite often, Mike and Carol will approach Alice for advice about the kids, while Alice is vacuuming or cooking. In this way, Alice functions like the housewives of the 1950s. I argue that her housework signifies love and concern to those around her, thus indicating to them opportunities for advice. Alice's needs, like the 1950s housewives' needs, are almost never discussed explicitly, though, making her character exist solely to serve the other characters. However, again like the 1950s characters, she does this happily, so I would argue that Alice functions like Hazel as an equal member of the family: without fulfillment on some level, Alice's housework would bring to the fore the menial, task-oriented qualities of her work. Instead, her housework signifies authority, as family members seek her out in these moments of self-sacrificing service to help guide their own lives. Alice shows a type of strength in understanding her role of service to an architect and a housewife, who has almost no housekeeping duties, yet persists to help in ways that exceed her job description because she is committed to meeting the preservative demands of others.

CONCLUSION

In many ways, housework in the 1960s furthers the trends established in television shows of the 1960s. With the exception of a few characters, most housework in these shows functions to signify the qualities of maternal practice—preservation and love—but in the 1960s, we have examples of what housework becomes when it is removed from these qualities. The drudgery of the work is immediately exposed, and housework quickly becomes menial, meaningless, and task-oriented. Surprisingly, though, even when the performers of housework are male, unrelated, young, or supernatural, television signifies housework most often as an act that is inherently loving and consequently fulfilling. The 1960s also contributed new representations of housework, as it is used explicitly as punishment in *The Patty Duke Show*, as self-worth in *The Andy Griffith Show* and *Mayberry R.F.D.*, as self-restraint in *Bewitched*, as humanity in *I Dream of Jeannie*, as commitment in *Here's Lucy*, as common ground with the external world in *The Munsters* and *The Addams Family*, as courage in *Mayberry R.F.D.*, and as authority in *Hazel* and *The Brady Bunch*.

Most important, the 1960s brought variety to what is often considered stale and homogenous television in the 1950s, as shows provided new definitions for family, which in turn offered new representations of housework. Presented in this decade is a diversity of household models that included all-male families, female heads of household, servant family members, father-son-housekeeper arrangements, and bachelor fathers, in addition to the escapist shows, with witches, genies, monsters, and space cars. Still, almost every episode of each series included housework in its plot on some level, and most shows represented these housekeeping activities with similar inherent qualities of love, sacrifice, and strength, activities that actively center the performer of these tasks. Regarding these activities as maternal practice provides common ground among these visual texts, connects 1960s characters to those of other decades, and imbues housekeeping activity with new significance and meaning.

NOTES

1. Humphreys, "Supernatural Housework," 109.
2. Marc, *Comic Visions*, 117.
3. Betty Friedan, *The Feminine Mystique*. Tenth Anniversary Edition (New York: W.W. Norton & Company, Inc., 1974), 254.
4. Douglas, *Where the Girls Are*, 130.
5. Marc, *Comic Visions*, 128.

6. Lynn Spigel, *Welcome to the Dreamhouse: Popular Media and Postwar Suburbs* (Durham: Duke UP, 2001), 117.

7. Douglas, *Where the Girls Are*, 126.

8. An example of this popular interpretation is Susan J. Douglas's work *Where the Girls Are.*

9. Leibman, *Living Room Lectures,* 205. Jane Wyatt says, "Mom always had to be around with nothing to do . . . just to say 'wash your hands.'"

10. Betty Friedan, "Television and the Feminine Mystique," *TV Guide: The First 25 Years*, J.S. Harris, ed. (New York: New American Library, 1980), 97.

11. Hesse-Biber and Carter, *Working Women in America*, 179, 182.

12. Ibid., 179.

13. Leibman, *Living Room Lectures,* 218.

14. Ibid., 217.

15. Ibid., 129.

16. Douglas, *Where the Girls Are,* 133.

17. Marc, *Comic Visions*, 117.

18. Friedan, *The Feminine Mystique*, 251.

19. Leibman, *Living Room Lectures,* 193.

20. Hesse-Biber and Carter, *Working Women in America*, 180.

21. Douglas, *Where the Girls Are*, 134.

22. Marc, *Comic Visions*, 78.

Chapter 4

Televised Housework in the 1970s

As the 1960s came to a close, television began to eliminate the shows of dreams, magic, and fantasies—plots which were considered increasingly ridiculous toward the end of the decade—and enter into a period of what it considered to be realistic representation. Even though the 1960s domestic sitcom had redefined what constitutes "family" through its unique interpretations of household models, almost all of the shows still involved the same idyllic white suburban America so prevalent in the 1950s—the 1960s just muddled it through monsters, witches, genies, and deserted islands. However, as Marc reveals, "With the successes in the 1970s of shows such as *All in the Family*, *The Mary Tyler Moore Show*, *The Jeffersons*, *Rhoda*, and *Alice*, the genre would rediscover its own roots in ethnic humor and urban settings."[1] Since visual cultures, including the televised image, communicate what society thinks of itself, as Barthes claims, America was acknowledging its own diversity in television of the 1970s.

Whereas we find many changes from the 1960s with more shows involving single working women, families of color, working-class families, and apartment-settings in the 1970s, we see almost no male domestic labor. Depictions of men performing housework had already decreased in the 1960s from the 1950s—a surprising discovery considering the 1950s is perhaps the most criticized decade with regard to the strict dichotomy of dominant, public male roles and marginalized, private female roles in the home. In the 1960s, male domestic labor diminishes greatly, and certainly involves fewer husbands and fathers doing housework, but the decade still includes popular shows like *My Three Sons*, *Gilligan's Island*, *Family Affair*, and *The Munsters*, that depict men performing housework. In the 1970s, however, other than the occasional male pouring a drink, males performing housework becomes an almost non-existent televised image.

This study finds it particularly interesting that while 1950s television is regarded by some scholars as "patriarchal hegemony" where "dad rules the roost,"[2] and "men never attempt any of the chores on their own,"[3] housework—an activity of service—is performed by men more often in the 1950s than in shows of the 1960s and 1970s. This likely has something to do with feminism, as Douglas says that by the early 1970s, "the entertainment media were trying to figure out how to capitalize on feminism while containing it."[4] Perhaps one way of accomplishing this is through the juxtaposition of more powerful and diverse female characters, who outwardly profess authority and independence, but who television "contains" through constant, unaided housework—a finding that becomes disturbingly obvious when placed beside the visual texts of the 1950s and 1960s. Just as magic and fantasy disguised some of the sexism of 1960s television—statements like Tony Nelson's "I'm an astronaut, not a housekeeper," for example, in *I Dream of Jeannie* were more palatable because we knew Jeannie could send him to space for good if she wanted to—the prevalence of single, career-minded, powerful women in the 1970s disguises the increase in households where the female alone performs the housework—it tempers the explicit message of 1970s television that housework is for women, not for men. I am not arguing that women perform more housework in television of the 1970s, but rather that more shows have females performing these tasks alone, without assistance, while men perform no housework and receive total assistance. It is depictions of housework such as these that contribute to scholarly assessments like Douglas's, claiming that "despite the superficial appearance of change on TV with shows like *The Mary Tyler Moore Show* and *Police Woman*, the medium was as sexist as, possibly even more sexist, than in the days of . . . *I Love Lucy*."[5]

It is also likely the lack of televised male domestic labor in the 1970s has some connection to the antiauthoritarian nature of baby boomer culture. Many baby boomers had been reared within a family structure where the father was frequently absent due to long hours at work; thus, the centrality of father in 1950s visual culture is not depicted in most televised families of the 1970s.[6] Visual culture also influenced and was influenced by the 1970s opinions regarding marriage and children, as by the start of the decade, one third of college-age Americans were rejecting marriage and having children.[7] According to Kutulas, television's influence on these sentiments was intense, as "television stereotypes symbolized much of what they rebelled against. Young women feared becoming like June Cleaver—sweet, servile, and invisible, vacuuming in her pearls and high heels."[8] In an effort to avoid this version of mother, young females of the 1970s were drawn to shows involving independent, career women who appeared on the surface to be more self-serving than previous televised females.

At the very least, however, these ideas—the significance of representation's meaning and connection to its society—were a part of the American consciousness by the 1970s. Whereas television was still considered popular entertainment, it was no longer *just* entertainment, and this, as Douglas maintains, is a significant shift that occurs, particularly with women, by the 1970s:

> What was different, however, about the 1970s was that now millions of women had a sense that it was their right and responsibility to deconstruct these images even as they felt their pull. Almost every pseudofeminist gambit on television . . . produced a host of public analyses and attacks by women who agreed that imagery and symbolism mattered to our everyday lives . . .⁹

Considering housework is depicted on some level and in some way by most episodes in almost every television series of this decade, it is an important part of the "imagery and symbolism" being deconstructed by viewers. Housework indeed changes in the 1970s, and in some ways, this decade brings to the fore what Friedan regarded as the drudgery of housework, but even within this framework, I argue, these women show strength first and foremost through the preservative nature of their domestic labor, as they function as the active, rather than passive, centers of their homes. This analysis of housework representations in the 1970s includes the following fifteen television series:

The Partridge Family (1970–1974)
The Mary Tyler Moore Show (1970–1977)
All in the Family (1971–1979)
Maude (1972–1978)
Good Times (1974–1979)
Happy Days (1974–1984)
Rhoda (1974–1978)
The Jeffersons (1975–1985)
Laverne and Shirley (1976–1983)
Tabitha (1976–1978)
Soap (1977–1981)
Mary Hartman, Mary Hartman (1976–1977)
Three's Company (1977–1984)
Diff'rent Strokes (1978–1986)
Benson (1979–1986)
The Facts of Life (1979–1988)

THE PARTRIDGE FAMILY (1970–1974)

The Partridge Family aired for four years on ABC and depicted a widowed mother, Shirley Partridge (Shirley Jones), and her five children, Keith Douglas (David Cassidy), Laurie (Susan Dey), Danny (Danny Bonaduce),

Tracy (Suzanne Crough), and Christopher (Brian Forster), as they form a pop band, record albums, and perform. *The Partridge Family*, in a way, serves as a final example of the escapist shows of the 1960s. While it doesn't involve magic, as Marc notes, it is still a "remarkable 'the future has arrived' vision of the American family as a pop-music act."[10] Furthermore, it is one of the few examples from the 1970s of housework that is shared. Since Shirley is a single mother, the entire family contributes to the upkeep of the home and family. This is significant because it contributes to a trend established in the 1960s and discussed previously. When women are in charge of their households, and the males, with regard to roles of authority, are absent, the women and their children share the housework. This is true of the 1960s programs *The Lucy Show*, with a household run by two women, one widowed and one divorced, and *Here's Lucy*, with a household run by a single widow. Now, in the 1970s, we have Shirley Partridge, a widow with five children, all of whom share in the household duties. Yet, when males are depicted as widowers, as in *My Three Sons*, *The Andy Griffith Show*, and *Mayberry R.F.D.*, for example, they have women or family members come to their rescue to care for their home, or they hire housekeepers. The housework is no easier to accomplish for a single female than for a male, yet television depicts it as such. The connoted message, as Barthes called it, is that society expects women to continue running their homes as usual, even when they lose their husbands and absorb the added pressures of breadwinning and single-parenting, while widowed men should expect an aunt, a grandfather, or a housekeeper to move in and assume all of the household duties, so that his life remains as unchanged as possible. This assessment is fair, but when regarding housework as maternal practice, the fact that more single women perform it than men reflects a strong female desire to preserve life—a desire that is logical, intuitive, and a sign of strength. Whether television intended to or not, this contradiction implies a strength in female characters that is not present in the males—a strength that takes life as it comes and, as Aunt Bee says, "charges it in the raw." *The Partridge Family* is one of several shows in the 1970s that will further this dichotomy. Most important, though, it highlights the role of housework in deconstructing the televised image, as it reveals the strict binary oppositions that persist in original forms in new decades.

The egalitarian nature of the Partridge household is established in the first few episodes of the series. Shirley narrates that while she was working, "the kids all pitched in to run the house." As they eventually form a band and begin performing, she describes the newness of her role in the spotlight, claiming that the only time previously she had taken a bow was for a pot roast. The show is using this dialogue centered on housework to juxtapose Shirley's old life as housewife and new life as performer. In the episode "The Sound of Money," when the family finally makes it to California to begin a life as a

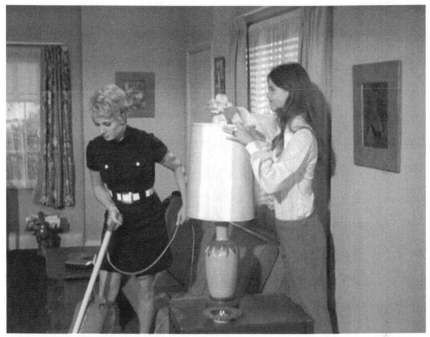

Figure 4.1 *The Partridge Family, Season One,* "The Sound of Money," © CPT Holdings, Inc., Courtesy Sony Pictures Television.

musical act, they immediately rear-end a car in a traffic accident. The man in the car wants to sue them and claim back injury. The Partridge family decides to move in with him and "take care" of him. The show presents an extensive montage of housework, where all family members are depicted vacuuming, dusting, and wiping. The man consequently grows to love the family and decides to drop the suit.

Housework functions here as both manipulation and as loving service. It is consistent with two trends I've identified. Like the shows *Hazel, I Love Lucy,* and *Petticoat Junction,* characters use housework to achieve an end result they don't feel they can achieve without the housekeeping activities. Housework is used to motivate others to give them what they want or need. In *The Partridge Family,* though, this is not presented as manipulation in a negative way, as the family appears to serve this man in earnest—to preserve his life from a back injury in the most literal way, by taking care of him. In *I Love Lucy,* Lucy is often depicted as using housework to convince Ricky to acquiesce and give her what she wants. The Partridge family use it here because both they cannot afford to pay the man and they genuinely care about his recovery.

Most important, the entire Partridge family exemplifies characteristics this study recognizes in almost all performers of housework, mostly female, analyzed in this study. It takes strength to respond to a wrongdoing, condescension, ridiculous expectations, sexism, etcetera, through acts of kindness and service. This is precisely the strength the housewife has shown over these decades, and in this episode, we see that strength in Shirley and her children. They suspect the man is not really injured, just as many housewives suspect their husbands can perform laundry and cooking by themselves, but instead of feeling bitter or mistreated, they respond with a strength inherent in serving others—which is precisely how housework functions. Therefore, in *The Partridge Family*, housework signifies preservative love, selflessness, maturity, and most important, equality, as the show depicts it as the most significant indicator of the egalitarian model of this household.

THE MARY TYLER MOORE SHOW (1970–1977)

The Mary Tyler Moore Show aired for seven years on CBS and presents a never-married, independent career woman Mary Richards (Mary Tyler Moore) and her best friend/upstairs neighbor Rhoda Morgenstern (Valerie Harper). Mary moves to Minneapolis alone, takes a job as an associate producer at a news station, and rents an apartment by herself. The show establishes Mary's relationship with her home and with Rhoda through housework. When Mary initially decides to rent her particular apartment, Rhoda is already in there, claiming the place is hers because she has already washed the windows and cleaned the carpets. Rhoda assumes her housework equals ownership, and even though these are depictions of two career-minded, independent women, housework is signified as the only language they speak as women. Rhoda wants Mary's apartment, so in order to take it from her before she moves in, she believes this can be achieved by cleaning it, as if the activity of housework places the "rented" tag on a home. The connoted message is that women communicate their needs through housework. In other words, instead of communicating verbally her desire for the apartment, Rhoda cleans it.

Like Lucy in *The Lucy Show* and *Here's Lucy*, and Shirley Partridge in *The Partridge Family*, Mary Richards works outside of the home. Therefore, much of the show occurs at Mary's place of work, following a similar format as *The Dick Van Dyke Show*. However, unlike Rob Petrie, who comes home to a housekeeping wife, Mary must also perform her own housekeeping duties. Much of her housework is implied, as she regularly comes home with an arm full of groceries or prepares a cup of tea for a guest. But if we compare her character to the characters of similar shows featuring males, such as *Family Affair* or *Bachelor Father*, we find that the single, career-minded male always makes enough money to hire a housekeeper, while the single, career-minded female barely makes enough to get by and must maintain her home entirely by herself. Whereas Mary's character might initially signify change for women in the power structures identified through television, with Mary answering to and serving only herself within the home, shows such as this also function to emphasize the effects of the wage gap in reality for women, in addition to the minimized employment opportunities for educated women. In *Family Affair*, Bill Davis is a civil engineer and in *Bachelor Father*, Bentley Gregg is an attorney, yet Mary Richards moves to a new city to seek employment as a secretary and, by chance, is hired as an associate producer at a news station. In other words, television communicates what society things of itself, and when network executives decided viewers were ready for a show featuring a single, independent woman, this character was *not* seeking employment as an engineer or attorney, but rather as a secretary. Because of her employment status and the wage gap, Mary cannot afford a housekeeper, and like the previously discussed widowed characters, she is expected to pull double duty, performing both at work and in the home—something her bachelor counterparts are not expected to do. Thus, in *The Mary Tyler Moore Show*, housework functions as both an indicator of employment inequalities and the wage gap, in addition to signifying a form of communication and ownership for women.

ALL IN THE FAMILY (1971–1979)

All in the Family aired for eight years on CBS and depicted working-class bigot Archie Bunker (Carol O'Conner), housewife Edith (Jean Stapleton), their married daughter Gloria (Sally Struthers), and son-in-law Michael (Rob Reiner). *All in the Family*'s contribution to visual culture was substantial. As Kutulas claims, it "appeared, sending shockwaves because of its rendering of a family decidedly unlike the Cleavers. . . Archie expects to be the patriarch of the family, expects the attendant status and power . . . Even though his wife offers up the trapping of his power (beer and chair), he is clearly not the lord and master of his castle."[11] Edith's character functions in total service to Archie, as she prepares all meals, retrieves items when he demands them, and keeps the house in order. Archie does not do any housework, and in addition to the strict binary oppositions the show creates through Edith's and Archie's characters, it also furthers the idea that, as Hesse-Biber and Carter claim, housework "is viewed not as labor but as matter-of-course feminine activity."[12] The show makes explicit the idea that Edith is responsible for the housework because she is the female. For example, in the episode "Archie Gives Blood," Edith's dialogue addresses the housewife's never-ending work week when she thinks she is coming down with a cold: "It's okay if he gets a cold. He's the husband. He can just take a day off and I'll be running up and down stairs all day. I'm the wife. I can't take time off. I can't go to bed." Similarly, in a later episode "Gloria's Pregnancy," Archie remembers helping Edith with certain child-rearing tasks. He asks her, "When Gloria was a baby and crying in the middle of the night, who got up with her?" Edith says, "I did." He continues, "No, I mean when she would cry like four and five times a night?" Edith responds, "I did." Archie says, "Well, then who got up to say 'Edith, the baby's crying?'" Edith says, "That was you." These examples not only further the idea that housework and child-rearing in the Bunker household are Edith's responsibility, but also that Archie remembers and views his role as that of a helper, when actually, Archie's "husband care," a term Hesse-Biber and Carter say "refers to the difference between housework generated and housework done by husbands"[13] is substantial—even more so than is typically depicted on television.

Interestingly, even though Edith's character maintains similarities to the televised housewives of the 1950s—she actively performs housework and most of her action centers on her housekeeping activities—*All in the Family* presents a model of household management that seems very different from previous models. Archie does not help Edith with even the smallest of tasks, a trend that begins in 1960s television. But Archie's character adds nuance to this trend through his constant criticisms of Edith's housework. Archie regularly criticizes the very work that enables him to function comfortably—the very housework his lifestyle *needs* performed for him. Edith performs her housework as actively, visibly, and cheerfully as other housewife characters, despite Archie's regular criticisms and resistance to helping. But because Archie never helps, never loves on her while she is working, and never thanks her—all of which is part of the comedy of the show and of Archie's characterization—it is tempting to read Edith's service as an indication of weakness instead of strength, to infer that she absorbs Archie's treatment out of an inability to do anything about it. However, Edith's housework signifies the same desire to preserve and the same strength embodied by other characters, as she finds fulfillment in being *needed* by Archie. Just as Aunt Bee needed to feel needed in *The Andy Griffith Show* and *Mayberry R.F.D.*, Edith is fulfilled by performing tasks that Archie *needs* for survival, yet will not perform himself, and the more he criticizes her, the more she knows she is doing a job others couldn't do. This reality empowers her, and in this regard, Edith Bunker is the very picture of strength.

Another trend established in the 1970s that I believe more effectively contributes to housework being "viewed not as labor but as matter-of-course feminine activity," is the function of housework as female therapy. In this decade, we begin to see representations of housework that involve females being soothed, calmed, and comforted by housekeeping duties. I have been regarding activities of maternal practice as imbuing strength, but it is not until the 1970s that visual culture reveals them also therapeutic. When Edith is worried or overly excited about something, she will perform extra, often unnecessary housework to calm herself. For example, when Gloria finds out she is pregnant, Edith immediately begins unnecessarily cleaning out the cabinet below the sink because she doesn't want poisonous substances in reach of children—children who will not be crawling around for another year. Similarly, when Gloria has a miscarriage and is upstairs with the doctor, Mike comes down to tell Edith she is okay. Edith says, "I've been so worried, this is the fifth pot of tea I've made, and I scrubbed the sink nine times."

Housework functions as a naturally therapeutic activity for Edith. Unfortunately, this depiction also furthers the misconception that keeping house is a natural female attribute—something so natural that Edith must turn to it to feel normal again. Housework is represented as therapy for women throughout the 1970s, and we will revisit this trend later with shows such as *Rhoda* and *Mary Hartman, Mary Hartman*.

Figure 4.2 *All in the Family, Season One,* **"Gloria's Pregnancy,"** © ELP Communications Inc., Courtesy Sony Pictures Television.

MAUDE (1972–1978)

Maude ran for six years on CBS and is a spin-off of *All in the Family*, where the character Maude (Bea Arthur) plays Edith's cousin. In *Maude*, Maude Findlay is an outspoken matriarch who lives with her fourth husband, Walter Findley (Bill Macy), and adult divorced daughter, Carol Traynor (Adrienne Barbeau). The character Maude involves a unique juxtaposition of outspoken, politically minded, liberal, feminist, and housewife/caretaker. She is a very different housewife character from what television depicts previously. Maude's home is decorated with abstract art, something 1960s television such as *Bewitched* placed in the male's place of employment, instead of the home, to indicate the male sphere of intelligence. However, we find it in the home in *Maude*, an immediate indication that Maude's character is going to represent both male and female qualities. (Incidentally, this is furthered by a reoccurring joke in the series involving Maude's low voice. When she answers the phone, she often corrects the person on the other end, telling them she is *Mrs.* not *Mr.* Findlay.) And even though he never does any real housework, Walter will often pour Maude a drink, and she will converse with him over hard liquor.

Figure 4.3 *Maude, Season One,* "Maude Meets Florida," © ELP Communications Inc., Courtesy Sony Pictures Television.

At the same time, Maude is the caretaker of the home, and she regularly uses housework in the same way other television housewives use it, even though she herself is a very different housewife representation. First, the introduction of the show depicts Maude opening the front door of the home and smiling, echoing the intros of shows like *The Donna Reed Show* and *Leave It to Beaver* from the 1950s, but *Maude*'s housewife character is almost nothing like Donna Stone and June Cleaver in personality. However, her housework *is*. In fact, housework is what connects *Maude*'s version of domesticity to its domestic sitcom predecessors. For example, Maude will often set the table, cook, or wash dishes with her daughter Carol as a moment to enjoy conversation with her, and Carol approaches Maude for advice during her housekeeping activities, thus indicating Carol, like the televised families of the 1950s, recognizes the inherent love in her mother's maternal practice and regards these activities as opportunities for further emotional support. When there are issues the family does not want to discuss, as in the episode "Maude and the Psychiatrist," they also use housework as a distraction, like talking about the food or clearing the table instead of mentioning the controversial topic of Carol seeing a psychiatrist.

Maude's most important contribution to this study, however, is revealed through her relationship with her housekeeper, Florida Evans (Esther Rolle) in the first few seasons. In the episode "Maude Meets Florida," Maude requests a black maid specifically. In preparing for the housekeeper to come over and be interviewed, Maude is frantically cleaning the house. She doesn't want the new housekeeper to see a "disorderly" house. Walter interjects, claiming, "it isn't disorderly, it's dirty." Maude's need to present a clean home to her prospective housekeeper reflects the ideals of domesticity put forth by the 1950s—ideals that had somewhat relaxed in the 1960s with shows like *Here's Lucy*. More important, though, it reflects the female's desire to impress other females through her domestic sphere, as is depicted in *The Goldbergs*, *The Andy Griffith Show*, and *I Dream of Jeannie*, for example.

Housework signifies self-worth for many of these characters, and even though Maude is an outspoken feminist, focused on equality, she still uses the cleanliness of her home as a way to find common ground with other women, as a way of communicating to other women that she is like them—that she is "normal" because she keeps a clean house. And after having a series of disputes with Florida once she is hired, mainly because Maude refuses to let her do any work or use the back door because she is black and Maude does not want her to feel marginalized, the two women become friends and resolve their differences over a final argument regarding the best ways to clean a house.

As Maude suspects, housework functions as their common ground, as their form of communication. I believe this occurs because of the inherent strength

Figure 4.4 *Maude, Season One,* "Maude Meets Florida," © ELP Communications Inc., Courtesy Sony Pictures Television.

of performing preservative, life-sustaining, housekeeping activities that is recognized by these female characters—*that* is what these women actually have in common. Housework merely serves as the signifier of this shared understanding of strength, both in representation and in reality.

GOOD TIMES (1974–1979)

Good Times aired for five years on CBS and is a spin-off of *Maude*, as Esther Rolle's popularity on *Maude* resulted in the creation of the show *Good Times*. *Good Times* depicts the Evans family, Florida (Esther Rolle) and James (John Amos), and their three children, James Jr. "J.J." (Jimmie Walker), Thelma (BerNadette Stanis), and Michael (Ralph Carter). What is unique about Florida in this show, as she and Thelma perform most housekeeping tasks, is that she does not perform much of her housework throughout scenes or during dialogue, as many televised housewives do. She often enters with a laundry basket or finishes stirring the oatmeal as a scene begins, but when she is with the family and the dialogue begins, she stops performing housework and focuses on the conversation. Furthermore, she eats when the family eats, and even though she serves them, she does not spend the scene moving around in service, as is depicted with Harriet Nelson and Edith Bunker, for example. Florida's housework is depicted as being secondary to other types of service to her family, mainly conversation, listening, and advice. *Good Times* provides an example of the "invisibility" of housework, considering much of the actual housekeeping duties are not seen but inferred. It is important to emphasize, though, that the invisibility of the housework does not function to remove Florida from scenes. In other words, she does not excuse herself to perform tasks. It is implied that the scenes are occurring between, before, or after her housekeeping activities. Housework does, however, function to create strict gender distinctions in *Good Times*, as Florida frequently orders her daughter Thelma to get in the kitchen and do the dishes, but she does not make the same demands of her sons.

HAPPY DAYS (1974–1984)

Happy Days aired for ten years on ABC and depicts an idealized version of life in the 1950s. Characters include father Howard Cunningham (Tom Bosley), his wife Marion (Marion Ross), their son Richie (Ron Howard), and daughter Joanie (Erin Moran). Since the premise of the show involves an idyllic version of postwar life, domesticity is depicted with the same attributes highlighted by scholars of domestic sitcoms of the 1950s. Regarding mid-century television, Leibman points out, "Mother's potential narrative and emotional dominance in the kitchen is undercut by the fact that she is always standing and serving, and thus too active to participate in familial discussion."[14] In her analysis of June Cleaver from *Leave It to Beaver*, she also claims that the housewife character is forever asking the husband to explain the behavior of the children,[15] and that she consequently serves as dad's "moral backup." Whereas, I don't see this dominating the shows of the 1950s, since *Happy Days* presents its own idea of the 1950s, this description seems to dominate Marion's model of domesticity. Marion will miss eating with the family because she is too busy serving, a quality that makes her very different from concurrent examples such as Florida in *Good Times*, and even when she has a plate full of food ready to eat, she will ask others if they want more before she begins eating herself. This activity typically removes her from the table and the conversation. Consequently, after these scenes, Marion is left to question Howard as she clears the table, saying, "What should we do about Richie, Howard?" Similarly, in the episode "The Lemon," Richie is out late, so Howard goes looking for him. When they return and Marion has been waiting at home worried, she immediately excuses herself to make hot chocolate, while Richie explains his actions to his father. *Happy Days* provides a depiction of housework consistent with critical assessments of television in the 1950s: housework functions to remove Marion from many of the important familial discussions, leaving her to ask parenting questions of Howard.

Happy Days highlights another important critical assessment regarding gender and television. In her seminal work *Make Room for TV*, Spigel mentions how television complicated "normative conception of masculinity and femininity." Because females were depicted as such productive workers within the home, television transferred feminine notions of passivity to the males in the family.[16] Before and after dinner, Marion will be in the kitchen while Howard watches television, but more interestingly, Marion will call her daughter Joanie in to help, specifically telling her to perform kitchen duties instead of watching television with her father. In other words, whereas in *Good Times*, Florida tells Thelma to get in the kitchen, Marion's dialogue actually distinguishes between the active task of housework—what Joanie *should* be doing—and the passive activity of watching television—the proper place for Howard. Since most scenes of *Happy Days* occur within the domestic sphere, the women are often depicted, through housework, as the producers, the productive workers, the preservers of life, and consequently, the men assume passive roles of leisure in front of the television. *Happy Days* adds nuance to this by going beyond depictions of women fetching beers for men seated in front of the television set, as in *All in the Family*, by addressing television's inversion of masculine/active-feminine/passive norms explicitly through scenes such as this.

RHODA (1974–1978)

Rhoda ran for four years on CBS as a spin-off of *The Mary Tyler Moore Show*, where Rhoda Morgenstern (Valerie Harper) is Mary's best friend in Minneapolis. In *Rhoda*, she moves back to New York City and lives with her sister Brenda (Julie Kavner). Additional characters include Rhoda's parents, Ida (Nancy Walker) and Martin (Harold Gould), and her boyfriend/husband Joe (David Groh). Housework serves a unique function in the show because the series presents a lead female, who is initially single, then married, and then single again. When Rhoda lives with her sister, the extent of their housework involves pulling down bowls from cabinets and filling them with cereal and milk. They perform only the housework they each need personally to survive. During this time, Rhoda is on unemployment and looking for work as a window display designer. In the episode "The Lady in Red," her father Martin brings over groceries and dinner cooked by her mother because they are worried about Rhoda's finances. Thus, in these early episodes, housework is depicted as something that occurs more often at Ida's and Martin's apartment than Rhoda's and Brenda's. Still, it is essential to make the point that Rhoda and Brenda are two more examples of single females on television who are responsible for their own housework, as they, unlike similar male characters, cannot afford housekeepers.

In Ida's and Martin's apartment, Ida is extraordinarily committed to and comforted by maintaining a clean apartment, to the extent that she covers her furniture and lamps with plastic to avoid getting them dirty. Ida's housework differs greatly from her daughters,' a disconnect Kutulas claims is central to 1970s television. "Television housewives of the 1970s fervently believed in what June Cleaver did all day, so fervently, that they wanted their daughters to be like her and them. There was a constant tug-of-war on shows like *Rhoda* between those mothers and their daughters."[17] For Ida, housework and cleanliness are depicted as therapy—something she needs to do to feel human—much like Edith in *All in the Family*. This is first revealed in the episode "Parent's Day." Ida finds out that Rhoda is dating someone seriously, but she has not introduced him to the family. To comfort herself, Ida stays up all night vacuuming, until Martin encounters her. She claims to be vacuuming because she is upset over not having met Joe yet. Ida's desire to preserve, to engage in maternal practice, involves more than housework, as she seeks to establish important lifelong relationships for her daughter as well; she sees her role in doing so as being directly connected to the cleanliness of her home.

We see her connection to housework initially through these scenes, but Ida's affection for housework is depicted later as going much deeper. Rhoda finally decides to introduce Joe to her parents, and asks that they have a casual, low-key dinner together without her mother's typical "fuss." In an effort to comply, Ida welcomes Joe over to their house and apologizes for the "mess," which is two newspapers left on the couch. Unfortunately, Martin immediately admits that Ida made him go out to buy the newspapers just to make the place look messy. Rhoda admits that when she was under their care, her mother was so neat they "never even had a morning and evening paper in the house at the same time." Then Rhoda notices they have removed the plastic from the furniture and lamps, but Ida pretends this means nothing and that she does very little housework in reality. This, of course, is turned into comedy when Rhoda exclaims, "the house is too quiet." Martin says it is because the plastic, which is normally covering all the furniture, isn't popping. Ultimately, Rhoda claims to want her mother to "be herself," and Ida subsequently opens the doors to the dining room, which has been formally set for about eighteen guests, all of whom begin to enter through the front door. At the end of the evening, after everyone has left, Martin asks Ida if she was upset that Joe wasn't Jewish. She replies, "Yeah, a little. But I'll be alright in a minute." At that point, she is off screen, but we hear her start the vacuum cleaner. The episode is bookended by Ida's use of housework as therapy. The show uses housework to signify the idea that women feel better, feel more like themselves, feel more "normal," through the process of cleaning and maintaining clean households. Whereas this study seeks to emphasize the strength that is inherent in the preservative qualities of housework, as I have mentioned before with *All in the Family*, and this depiction contributes to the misconception that housework is a natural female attribute, Ida's desire to preserve life is still central to her housekeeping activities.

Despite her mother's influences, Rhoda is depicted as a woman who resists housework early in her marriage. In the episode "The Honeymoon," Rhoda and Joe are in bed after getting married, when she asks, "Do you want me to fix you breakfast?"—something the show rarely, if ever, depicts Rhoda doing in singlehood for herself. He replies, "No," and she says, "Ever? Hello happiness!" Later in the episode, Rhoda's parents come over for dinner, and Ida asks what Rhoda has fixed for her husband's first dinner? Rhoda goes over to the refrigerator, saying she was tired, and she pulls out a bucket of chicken that she picked up on the way home. Her resistance to housework is furthered in a later episode, "9-E Is Available," when one of Joe's ex-girlfriends visits their apartment. Rhoda invites her to stay for a drink, but when the ex-girlfriend requests vodka, Rhoda can't find any and claims they are out. The ex-girlfriend, who obviously knows Joe's apartment better than Rhoda, claims that is impossible and finds the vodka. Housework is used to establish ownership by these women, just as it is in *The Mary Tyler Moore Show*, when Rhoda attempts to stake claim to Mary's apartment because she has cleaned it. Additionally, housework is used to compete, as it is in shows like *The Goldbergs* and *Maude*, when the ex-girlfriend attempts to prove that she knows Joe more intimately by knowing his domestic sphere more intimately than Rhoda. After these episodes, however, Rhoda is depicted as cooking dinner for Joe every night, showing a distinct difference between her life as an independent woman and her life as a married woman. More to the point of this study, though, Rhoda is depicted as being happy serving Joe, adopting some of the maternal practices of her mother, thus furthering the point that, according to television, women are happier serving others than serving themselves, a point that, while disturbing, is ultimately a signification of great female strength.

THE JEFFERSONS (1975–1985)

The Jeffersons ran for ten years on CBS as a second spin-off of *All in the Family*, and depicts the Bunker's neighbors, the now wealthy Jefferson family of husband George (Sherman Hemsley), wife Louise (Isabel Sanford), and son Lionel (Mike Evans). The premise of the show involves the family's newfound wealth, as their dry-cleaning business, which began small, grows to be very successful, and they are able to afford a new "deluxe apartment" and luxuries they hadn't known before, like a maid. This new lifestyle changes Louise's role, as she has always been solely responsible for the care of the home. Now, George claims he just wants her to enjoy herself, so he hires a maid to handle the cooking and cleaning. *The Jeffersons* addresses explicitly Louise's loss of joy and purpose, when she is removed from her housekeeping duties. In the episode "Louise Feels Useless," Louise complains to a neighbor about how bored she is, claiming all she can do is sit in chairs and stare at walls all day. Later, her son Lionel asks her to stay out of his room, but she says she wants to clean it. He reminds her she cleaned it yesterday and it doesn't need to be cleaned again, which disappoints her. The next time she is with her neighbor again, she serves her tea and says she hates that her son doesn't need her anymore: "I got no reason for getting out of bed in the morning," she says. In the next scene, however, Louise is in the kitchen, with her apron on, cooking. She is depicted as being so happy and fulfilled through this activity that she is singing and dancing as she cooks. Lionel enters and comments on her explicit happiness.

Figure 4.5 *The Jeffersons, Season One,* **"Louise Feels Useless,"** © ELP Communications Inc., Courtesy Sony Pictures Television.

Obviously, episodes such as this tie Louise's self-worth directly to her housework, to her capacity to serve, to her desire to preserve the ones she loves. Like Aunt Bee in *The Andy Griffith Show* and Edith in *All in the Family*, their need to be needed surpasses any drudgery that may accompany the housework, and these women are depicted as believing their greatest achievements, their greatest contributions are possible in the home through their housework. As I have argued before, this trend has the unfortunate by-product of implying housekeeping is a natural attribute of women, but at the same time, this analysis recognizes the strength that is also implied in the dialogue, such as Louise's, when she states that housework—that service to one's family—gives her "a reason for getting out of bed in the morning." This depiction of the housewife as being completely fulfilled through servitude exemplifies an internal strength not often recognized in these female characters, and their housework specifically, signifies these qualities. Furthermore, Louise's characterization is perhaps one of the strongest examples on television of this commitment to and lifelong fulfillment through activities of maternal practice.

LAVERNE AND SHIRLEY (1976–1983)

Laverne and Shirley aired for seven years on ABC as a spin-off of *Happy Days* and starred Penny Marshall as Laverne De Fazio and Cindy Williams as Shirley Feeney. Like *The Mary Tyler Moore Show*, *Rhoda*, and later *Tabitha*, *Laverne and Shirley* depicts single, independent women, who, in this case, work in a bottling factory. The show serves as another example of working women who must pull double duty because they do not make enough money to hire housekeepers, versus similar single male characters who rarely perform their own housework because they are depicted as working in professions that pay higher wages and can afford to hire help. Laverne's and Shirley's housework, however, is minimal. In fact, their basement apartment is depicted as messy and cluttered, with clothes hanging in the living room and piles of books and magazines everywhere. Their kitchen is also small and cluttered, and all of their food is exposed, out in the open, instead of concealed in cabinets. When they eat, they usually grab a chair, stand on it, pull down a few cans of something, and pour the cans into bowls. This show's treatment of housework is very similar to that of *Rhoda*, which seems to indicate that television regards housework as something performed for others, not necessarily for oneself. Even though similar shows like *The Mary Tyler Moore Show* and *Tabitha* involve working women with cleaner apartments than *Laverne and Shirley* and *Rhoda*, they still do very little housework in these shows. Yet, when single men are able to hire housekeepers, as in *Family Affair*, *The Andy*

Griffith Show, Mayberry R.F.D., and later *Diff'rent Strokes*, the housekeepers are seen performing housework in every episode. The message seems clear, as far as television is concerned. Housework is performed and enjoyed only when it functions in the service of others, even when the "others" are unrelated and being served as a job. What this signification highlights are the self-sacrificial qualities of this type of work. Through these images, the connoted message claims we are not as concerned with the cleanliness of our domestic spheres or the quality of the food we eat when we are only serving ourselves; yet, when we transition to serve others, whether they are spouses, children, or employers, we begin to care and often become fulfilled by the quality of our housekeeping tasks—by our abilities to preserve life. This is a strength and fulfillment often seen in housewife characters, and then characters of multiple types, that isn't typically recognized in feminist scholarship.

TABITHA (1976–1978)

Tabitha ran for two years on ABC as a spin-off of *Bewitched*, where Tabitha is Samantha and Darrin Stephens's daughter. In this show, Tabitha

Figure 4.6 *Tabitha, Season One,* "Tabitha's Party," © CPT Holdings, Inc., Courtesy Sony Pictures Television.

(Lisa Hartman) is a single, independent, working woman, who has her mother's magical powers, but rarely uses them. Tabitha works as a production assistant for a television station, but like similar female characters of her era, Mary Richards and Rhoda Morgenstern, she makes a modest living and performs all of her own housework. The series doesn't last very long, and within those few episodes, Tabitha performs very little housework, but she is seen making her own meals and straightening up occasionally.

I include it in this study because it serves as another example of the single woman, who has a career, but is not depicted as earning a wage that can afford her a housekeeper. This furthers the assessment that men do not perform housework in the television shows of the 1970s, and even women who play career-driven roles, must be capable of maintaining their own housework, while similar male characters hire housekeepers.

SOAP (1977–1981)

Soap ran for four years on ABC as a parody of daytime soap operas. It depicts the families of two sisters, Jessica Tate (Katherine Helmond) and Mary Campbell (Cathryn Damon). The Tates are a wealthy family with a butler, Benson (Robert Guillaume), and the Campbells are a working-class family who perform their own housework. The show's plots oscillate between the lives of these two families. In the Tate household, Benson performs all of the cooking and cleaning, but he does so with a great deal of sarcasm and attitude, often claiming when he cooks, "If I don't like it, I don't make it." In this way, Benson interjects a bit of self-service into his service of others. In other words, he is only going to inconvenience himself to a certain extent in the service of the Tate family, and he draws the line at cooking meals he won't eat himself. Benson's dialogue here is very similar to the boundaries Bub set in his housekeeping activities on *My Three Sons*; he will clean the socks, but not fold them. In this way, Benson, and male characters like him, uses housework to make himself a part of the family by including himself in his service. Interestingly, with similar female housekeeper characters, such as Hazel in *Hazel*, Alice in *The Brady Bunch,* or Florida in *Maude*, they too are depicted as finding ways to connect and become a part of the family, but their methods typically involve conversation and advice—signs of emotional support. Benson joins himself to the family by including his own personal needs, explicitly through dialogue, in his service to others. Consequently, Benson's meals, such as Eggs Benedict in the first episode, are not liked when they are received. But Benson likes them, so it matters not what the family thinks.

Benson's disregard for the contentment of those he serves is so contrary to similar female housekeeper characters that it underscores the egregious differences in the way television regards the place and function of the female versus the male within the domestic sphere. Benson's approach almost renders him ineffective within the home—the family won't eat the food he "technically" made for himself—underscoring the message that perhaps Benson's proper place as a male is not in the kitchen because he does not inhabit the same desire to preserve that we have witnessed in female characters. Interestingly, when Benson's character returns later in the show *Benson*, he maintains his role as house manager, but his duties in the kitchen, for example, are stripped from his character, a point that reinforces this message further.

Whereas Benson keeps the Tate residence clean and orderly, the Campbell household is depicted very differently, as they manage their own cleaning and cooking. One example worth mentioning is the first episode, which uses housework to establish the discordant relationship between Burt Campbell (Richard Mulligan) and his stepson Danny Dallas (Ted Wass). In this scene, the men threaten each other by using food, going back and forth, attempting to make each threat scarier than the previous one. (Incidentally, while this depiction is much more violent, it maintains similarities to Laura and Rob Petrie's argument using liver in a pan on the stove in *The Dick Van Dyke*

Figure 4.7 *Soap, Season One,* **"Episode 1,"** © CPT Holdings, Inc., Courtesy Sony Pictures Television.

Show.) Danny says, "This is your head," as he crushes an egg in his hand, and Burt responds, "This is your neck," while he slices a banana. Danny squeezes raw meat and says, "This is your spine," and Burt takes a bite out of a fruit, saying, "This is your heart." Danny grabs the milk and begins stabbing it, saying, "This is your body."

The characters use the food and utensils—items that are typically used to sustain life and provide nourishment—to illustrate their hatred for each other, and meanwhile, they make a mess of the kitchen. They do not clean up the mess, and instead, allow Mary to enter with a mop and clean it, while they finish eating breakfast and leave. Their inability to understand the function of food and kitchen utensils is made explicit, thus intensifying gendered divisions within the home.

Housework is used to establish relationships, as well as to distinguish the differences between the Tate and Campbell households—two equally dysfunctional households on the inside that appear very different on the outside. When housework is depicted as being performed in the service of oneself, as it is with Benson refusing to cook anything he won't eat himself or Burt and Danny satisfying their desire to "get even" through their "food threats," it is often interpreted as being messy and unwelcomed. This reinforces television's message that selflessly serving others—regarding its life giving qualities—is a requirement for happy, effective housework, a trend visible also in *Green Acres* and later in *Mama's Family*.

MARY HARTMAN, MARY HARTMAN (1976–1977)

Mary Hartman, Mary Hartman aired for a year in syndication also as a soap opera parody, depicting the typical American housewife, Mary Hartman (Louise Lasser). Other characters include her husband Tom (Greg Mullavey), mother Martha Shumway (Dody Goodman), and sister Cathy Shumway (Debralee Scott). Since the show is a parody of the typical American housewife, Mary performs a great deal of housework and much of the show centers on housekeeping activities. Mary is almost always doing laundry or cooking during domestic scenes, and like Edith in *All in the Family* and Ida in *Rhoda*, *Mary Hartman, Mary Hartman* presents housework as therapy for Mary. In episode thirteen, when Mary's daughter Heather runs away from home, Mary claims to be worried. Her mother says, "You don't look worried, standing there cooking up a storm." Mary responds, "I cook when I'm worried!" Similarly, in episode eleven, when Tom doesn't come home over night, Mary is perpetually ironing. She says, "If I keep busy, the time goes faster." Mary is depicted as working through her difficult situations and being comforted by her housework.

Furthermore, the show upholds domesticity explicitly through dialogue, as well. In episode ten, Martha tries to comfort her daughters, claiming her mother always told her that "If you keep a neat house and cook wholesome meals, the Lord will take care of everything else." Martha's dialogue reinforces the male/public-female/private distinction and emphasizes the idea that the female's domestic sphere is not her *primary* concern, but should be her *only* concern.

Most important, *Mary Hartman, Mary Hartman* adds nuance to this study because Mary's kitchen includes a television set, and she often mops or irons while watching television.

This is significant because it is one of the only examples included in this study that reflects what Spigel discusses as an issue of great importance to network executives during the postwar era. Since the housewife is the target consumer of advertisers, her daily housework routine was considered in determining programming schedules, as network executives sought to find ways to draw the attention of housewives without disturbing their work. The television industry knew the housewife would prioritize her housework over

Figure 4.8 *Mary Hartman, Mary Hartman, Season One,* **"Episode 1,"** © ELP Communications Inc., Courtesy Sony Pictures Television.

watching television, so they desired effective approaches to navigating her labor-leisure choices during the day:

> Above all, women's leisure time was shown to be coterminous with their work time. Representations of television continually addressed women as housewives and presented them with a notion of spectatorship that was inextricably inter-twined with their useful labor at home . . . we can assume that women were able to adapt some of their [radio] listening habits to television viewing without much difficulty. However, the added impact of visual images ushered in new dilemmas that were the subject of profound concern, both within the broadcast industry and within the popular culture at large.[18]

Visual culture in general was faced with establishing effective methods for getting the housewife's attention, while simultaneously encouraging the importance of her housework—in other words, a desire for efficient housekeeping contributes to increased consumerism. *Mary Hartman, Mary Hartman* represents a housewife integrating labor and leisure by placing a television set in her kitchen so that she will not miss certain shows, while per-forming her daily tasks of maternal practice. The show reflects this practical solution to the actual housewife's labor-leisure dilemma—a solution Spigel mentions comes out of the print culture of the era:

> *Better Homes and Gardens* advised in 1949 that the television set should be placed in an area where it could be viewed, "while you're doing things up in the kitchen." Similarly in 1954, *American Home* told readers to put the TV set in the kitchen so that "Mama sees her pet programs. . . ." Via such spatial remedies, labor would not be affected by the leisure of viewing nor would viewing be denied by household chores.[19]

Mary Hartman, Mary Hartman is unique in that it is one of few shows depict-ing a housewife who implements this "spatial remedy," as Mary is a character who spends so much time performing housework in the kitchen that she must place a television there in order to catch her favorite programs and to perhaps provide entertainment during her tasks. Even though the show underscores the fulfilling qualities of Mary's housework—her care for husband and child is clear through her work—it simultaneously engages discourses of house-wife boredom through her constant television-viewing habits.

THREE'S COMPANY (1977–1984)

Three's Company ran for seven years on ABC and depicts three single room-mates, Janet Wood (Joyce DeWitt), Chrissy Snow (Suzanne Somers), and

Jack Tripper (John Ritter). The show does not portray a great deal of housework, but it is included here for one main reason. The two females, Janet and Chrissy, like the idea of Jack replacing their third roommate because he is learning to be a cook and the girls do not know how to cook. Like the show *Benson,* later *Three's Company* reveals a premise that involves a male being introduced specifically for his domestic knowledge, in this case cooking. However, in the first season, Jack is never really seen cooking. Certain scenes indicate that Jack is about to give Janet a cooking lesson, for example, but he never follows through. This point is reinforced later through *Benson,* but television in the 1970s does not depict men as doing housework, even when they claim to have these skills and use them often. This means if these male characters, like Jack, are cooking and cleaning in the story, television has decided these tasks, when performed by males, should be invisible in the plot, thus, in turn, automatically emphasizing the visibility of the female's domestic labor.

DIFF'RENT STROKES (1978–1986)

Diff'rent Strokes ran for eight years on ABC and depicts wealthy widower Phillip Drummond (Conrad Bain) and his daughter Kimberly (Dana Plato), who take in two African-American boys from Harlem, Arnold Jackson (Gary Coleman) and his older brother Willis (Todd Bridges). As with other shows featuring single white male leads, Mr. Drummond is wealthy and has a hired housekeeper, Mrs. Garrett (Charlotte Rae), who later leaves the show for her own spin-off *The Facts of Life.* Therefore, as with *Family Affair* and *The Andy Griffith Show,* the single white male lead, Mr. Drummond, is rarely seen performing any duties related to housekeeping. Mrs. Garrett is portrayed as a combination of previous televised housekeepers, Hazel from *Hazel* and Alice from *The Brady Bunch.* Like Hazel, Mrs. Garrett uses housework to manipulate and distract. When she doesn't want to listen to Mr. Drummond, she intentionally starts vacuuming while he is talking and claims innocently that she can't hear him.

She uses housework to remove herself from situations she does not want to be involved in. Like Alice, and like most of the televised housewives of the 1950s, Mrs. Garrett is always approached for advice while she is performing housework. While she is cooking dinner, Mr. Drummond asks her how he can make the boys feel more at home or what he should do about one of their problems, for example. Her housework actively centers her as the source of love, knowledge, and emotional support in the patriarchy of the Drummond household. In this way, as is revealed in the 1950s, television depicts housework as moments when the characters performing it are approachable—the

Figure 4.9 *Diff'rent Strokes, Season One,* "Movin' In," © ELP Communications Inc., Courtesy Sony Pictures Television.

assumption put forth is that they are already performing acts of service, so they will not mind serving further, in the form of advice and emotional support. This occurs over and over with the housewives of the domestic sitcoms in the 1950s and early 1960s, and with housekeeper characters like Hazel, Aunt Bee, Alice, and Mrs. Garrett.

Mrs. Garrett is also depicted as perpetually enjoying her housework. Similar to Louise Jefferson in *The Jeffersons*, when she is vacuuming, watering flowers, dusting, or icing cakes, for example, she is typically singing while she works—something television uses to signify happiness during labor. She is working in the service of others, individuals who are not her actual family, but she is depicted as being happy and fulfilled with this arrangement, and the show uses her housework to integrate Mrs. Garrett into the family. For example, when she tries to clear the table, often they won't let her because they want her to participate in their game night or other activities. In this way, the show oscillates between household management models of mutual effort and Mrs. Garrett as sole caretaker. Similarly, when she puts clothes away and cleans the boys' rooms, they will use those opportunities to scare her from the closet and integrate her into their play, showing their affection for her as a caretaker and playmate. All of this occurs during her activities of service, thus reinforcing the approachable qualities of a person working in service. The strength is inherent in Mrs. Garrett's ability to work happily in and be fulfilled by an arrangement that never truly addresses her own personal needs—her desire to meet the needs of her "family" is depicted as replacing personal needs.

BENSON (1979–1986)

Benson aired for seven years on ABC as a spin-off of *Soap*. It starred Robert Guillaume as Benson DuBois, who has been hired to run the household for widowed governor Eugene Gatling (James Noble) and his daughter Katie (Missy Gold). Benson serves as a male example of the Hazel, Alice, and Mrs. Garrett characters discussed previously in this study. This is important because Benson, though in charge of running the household, is depicted as doing very little actual housework, unlike the female housekeepers, who are perpetually and visibly engaged in active housework, to the extent that the qualities of their characters are often revealed by these activities. In fairness, Benson does have a cook and other help on staff, but it is strange that while we see similar female housekeepers perform regular housekeeping tasks, we rarely see Benson engage in any of these housekeeping activities, other than pouring the occasional cup of coffee for the Governor, at which time the Governor takes the opportunity to ask for Benson's advice.

This is a typical formula for housekeeper roles in the 1960s and 1970s. The families that hire them perpetually seek their advice, especially with regard to relationships and parenting, and the housekeepers are depicted as having all the answers. They always give the best advice.

In this regard, Benson is no different. He does add nuance to this formula, however, by offering unsolicited advice about all matters, personal and professional, private and public. For example, in early episodes, Benson realizes Eugene doesn't know what he is doing in his new position as the Governor, and he goes to Eugene's assistant, telling him he wants to give the Governor his ideas. The assistant refuses to allow this and tells Benson to focus on what he does best—"tuna fish ideas." Eventually, however, the Governor hears Benson's ideas and takes his advice. Benson's ideas solve the problem, and he, as a house manager, is now depicted as having much more responsibility than merely caring for the home.

This is significant because Benson is the only real example of a male housekeeper on television in the 1970s, and his character is immediately depicted as being *more* than just a housekeeper functioning within private matters. Similar female characters, such as Hazel, Alice, and Mrs. Garrett, are the

Figure 4.10   *Benson, Season One,* "Change," © CPT Holdings, Inc., Courtesy Sony Pictures Television.

voices of reason in their shows, with family members seeking their advice, thus centering their housework activities. But the show *Benson* sends the message that this formula will not suffice for a male housekeeper character, as Benson's common sense and intelligence would be wasted if applied only to the female sphere of domesticity, intuition, and self-sacrifice. Benson's advice is worthy of the male sphere of employment, logic, and intelligence. Furthermore, Benson is unable to get along with the female cook, who in actuality performs most of the visible housekeeping duties. Her character is presented as being completely illogical. For example, when Benson first arrives, he realizes that the family can save time and money by eating more leftovers. The cook insists she will not allow leftovers in the house—a completely illogical response to Benson's logical solution. She even threatens to kill him if leftovers are served in the house. Since Benson's female counterpart is depicted in this way, it makes his new rapport with the Governor more acceptable and understandable—we don't question why he is immediately able and allowed to advise the Governor. His relationship with the Governor also means he is responsible for more tasks of the male sphere, and fewer tasks, which the show depicts as menial, thus giving them to the illogical female cook, of the female sphere. This study must also question whether this aspect of housework is connected to Benson's lack of maternal practice. Benson's concern for the family is depicted as being less concentrated with preservation and more concerned with professional success and household harmony.

THE FACTS OF LIFE (1979–1988)

The Facts of Life ran for nine years on NBC as a spin-off of *Diff'rent Strokes*. Mrs. Garrett (Charlotte Rae) leaves the Drummond family to work as a housemother of an all-girls boarding school. The girls at the school include Blair Warner (Lisa Whelchel), Cindy Webster (Julie Anne Haddock), Natalie Green (Mindy Cohn), and Dorothy "Tootie" Ramsey (Kim Fields). Early episodes establish just how *needed* Mrs. Garrett is by the Drummond family from *Diff'rent Strokes*, as the episode "Rough Housing" includes these characters. They are visiting Mrs. Garrett, asking when she is going to return to them. Mr. Drummond says, "Ever since you left, everything has been upside down, topsy turvy." So even though he is a capable man with three children, they are unable to run their house efficiently without Mrs. Garrett. In shows with similar household models, like *The Partridge Family* and *Here's Lucy*, portraying a single female and children, all members of the household share the housework and function successfully. However, when this treatment is applied to the single male, as it is with Mr. Drummond, the management of the household is depicted as falling apart without a housekeeper.

Since this show involves a single female running a household of children, like similar shows, such as *The Partridge Family* and *Here's Lucy*, the housework is shared by everyone in the house. Mrs. Garrett regularly asks the girls to help out, and often, the girls are the ones to prod everyone into performing housework, as Nancy does in the episode "Like Mother, Like Daughter," saying, "Come on, girls; we've got to get back to work!" This episode, in particular, is important because even though the plot centers on Blair's relationship with her beautiful mother, it comments a great deal on housework and domestic ideals in general. In one scene, Mrs. Garrett is teaching Blair to sew. When she is surprised that Blair's mom did not teach her, Blair replies that her mother always said, "Beautiful women were not put on this earth to do menial tasks." Mrs. Garrett responds, "Nothing is menial if you feel good about yourself." This dialogue speaks directly to the point of this study that in a very genuine way, housework is depicted as making women feel good about themselves and that this is a sign of strength—the strength that is inherent in the preservative qualities of housework. I believe female viewers in reality connect with televised housework, and certainly with explicit statements such as Mrs. Garrett's, in deeply meaningful ways.

This episode does much more to glorify domesticity, though. Blair's mother spends much of the episode flirting with married men, and Blair decides she doesn't want to be anything like her mother when she grows up. Toward the end of the episode, though, Blair's mother exits the kitchen with most of the girls, wearing an apron and carrying a pot of food.

One of the girls asks, "Is that your mother in an *apron?*" Blair is pleasantly surprised, claiming, "Mother, you haven't cooked in years!" Nancy says, "You should have seen her. She was fantastic." To which Blair's mom replies, "Yeah, once they showed me the difference between the stove and the refrigerator . . . I thought it was time I started acting more like you." This episode depicts the mother maturing emotionally, as she ditches the self-serving behavior of flirting and takes on the self-sacrificing activity of cooking. Whereas the dialogue exaggerates her inexperience—it is implausible to say the least that a woman who successfully raised a daughter would need to be taught appliances—it highlights the satisfaction and fulfillment of serving others. When the mother finds herself searching for a way to connect with her daughter, the schoolgirls, who coexist by sharing household duties, teach her the value of self-sacrificing service. The mother reveals her

Figure 4.11 *The Facts of Life, Season One,* "Like Mother, Like Daughter," © ELP Communications Inc., Courtesy Sony Pictures Television.

domestic side to show her love for Blair. In this way, housework signifies love directly.

CONCLUSION

Television's message in the 1970s is clear: housework is gendered and women do the housework. Whereas several trends are established in this decade with regard to housework, this seems to be the most significant trend unique to this decade, as men are almost never seen performing housework in television of this decade. Even when a male is placed in the role of housekeeper, he is not depicted as doing frequent housework, but rather functioning often as a professional adviser to the patriarch. One potential reason for this involves the self-sacrificial qualities inherent in the housework discussed thus far. These 1970s shows signify that this self-sacrifice is more believable or perhaps realistic in female characters than in male characters, or that female characters regard a stronger connection between preservation and domestic activities. Regardless, the pattern is clear. When a show involves a single male—*Diff'rent Strokes* and *Benson* from this decade—the male has a housekeeper who maintains the home, and the children do not assist in the housekeeping duties. When a show depicts a single female—*The Partridge Family*, *Rhoda*, *The Mary Tyler Moore Show*, *Laverne and Shirley*, *The Facts of Life*, and *Tabitha*—she is responsible for the care of her own domestic sphere, in addition to any children present in the home. Furthermore, when the housekeeper is female, she is utilized as a source of comfort and guidance in the personal, private issues of her employer family, but when the housekeeper is male, his advice is accepted in both male and female realms, professional and personal, public and private.

Another trend revealed in this decade is housework functioning as therapy for women, thus contributing to the misconception that housekeeping is a natural female attribute. This is seen with Edith in *All in the Family*, when she relieves her concern for her daughter by scrubbing the sink nine times, for example, and with Ida in *Rhoda*, when she stays up all night vacuuming because she is nervous about Rhoda's new boyfriend. Even though it wasn't as explicit, this is also true of Louise in *The Jeffersons*, when she is depicted as feeling "normal" again after resuming some of her housekeeping duties. This raises an interesting point that television depicts these characters as feeling more like themselves, more "normal," when they are performing housework. This reinforces the idea that feeling "normal" for a female involves cooking and cleaning, signifying housekeeping as a natural female attribute. It also, however, underscores the female's impulse and ability to recognize and respond appropriately to vulnerability in others—a sign of strength, indeed.

The 1970s also uses housework to function as competition and ownership for women. In *The Mary Tyler Moore Show*, Rhoda attempts to stake claim to an apartment by cleaning it, and then later in her own show *Rhoda*, an ex-girlfriend appears to know Joe better by knowing his domestic sphere more intimately than Rhoda. And in *Maude*, Maude cleans her house in preparation for an interview with a maid so that the prospective housekeeper finds her to be a good housewife. Later, the two women argue—and consequently establish the foundational common ground that becomes their friendship—over the best methods for housekeeping.

While this decade presents some differences in representations in housework, it also depicts many similarities. In many of these shows, housework signifies the housewife's self-worth. It represents how intensely she needs to feel needed. This is revealed with Edith in *All in the Family*, Florida in *Good Times*, and especially Louise in *The Jeffersons*. Their housework—serving others who need their services—fulfills them on such a deep level that they cling to these activities. So even though this decade differs from previous decades through its return to "ethnic humor and urban settings," as Marc states, these qualities of housework connect television characters throughout these decades—the strength of the female characters to preserve life continues to underpin housework activities.

NOTES

1. Marc, *Comic Visions*, 154.
2. Leibman, *Living Room Lectures*, 118.
3. Ibid., 220.
4. Douglas, *Where the Girls Are*, 193.
5. Ibid., 200.
6. Kutulas, "Who Rules the Roost?" 54–55.
7. Ibid., 52–53.
8. Ibid., 52–53.
9. Douglas, *Where the Girls Are*, 194.
10. Marc, *Comic Visions*, 154.
11. Kutulas, "Who Rules the Roost?" 53.
12. Hesse-Biber and Carter, *Working Women in America*, 178.
13. Ibid., 180.
14. Leibman, *Living Room Lectures*, 130. This is located in the description for picture 16.
15. Ibid., 133.
16. Spigel, *Make Room for TV*, 96.

17. Kutulas, "Who Rules the Roost?" 55.

18. Spigel, *Make Room for TV*, 75.

19. Ibid., 89. See note 52 on page 209: Walter Adams and E.A. Hungerford, Jr., "Television: Buying and Installing It Is Fun; These Ideas Will Help," *Better Homes and Gardens*, September 1949, p. 38; *American Home*, December 1954, p. 39.

Chapter 5

Televised Housework in the 1980s

After a decade of sitcoms in the 1970s featuring various depictions of singles and their unique living arrangements—*The Mary Tyler Moore Show*, *The Partridge Family, Rhoda, Laverne and Shirley, Tabitha, Diff'rent Strokes, Three's Company*, and *Benson*—some of which continued well into the 1980s, it is no surprise that 1980s television responded by shifting away from a focus on singles and returning to traditional family-centered sitcoms. However, cultural scholars, such as Marc, claim this emphasis on traditional families did not reflect reality:

> By the last years of the 1980s, the nuclear-family sitcom was back on top of the ratings, even though, according to the Census Bureau, such families had become increasingly rare. . . . If the Andersons had been an idealized version of a "normal" American family, the Keatons of *Family Ties* and the Huxtables of *Cosby* were like families of gods in a nation of latchkey children.[1]

Ironically, while things like teen pregnancies, single parents, and divorce rates were on the rise in the 1980s, television shows promoting traditional family values and traditional nuclear families dominated the screen. Many of the most popular shows even include the word "family" in their titles—*Family Ties, Family Matters, Mama's Family*, for example. This likely has much to do with the popularity of cable television by the 1980s—a development begun in the 1970s that ended the hegemony of the three major networks ABC, CBS, and NBC. With so many options on cable, much of the adult wit that had dominated the sitcom in previous decades is lost in the 1980s, as television responds to a niche created by the diversity of options on cable by promoting sitcoms where, as Marc reveals, the "problems of raising those darned kids would rule the genre once again."[2]

Even though television's offerings become more diffuse with the popularity of cable in the 1980s, some trends are still identifiable with regard to housework. If I could label any of the four decades included in this study as being the decade of the "housekeeper sitcom," it would be the 1980s. Of the shows discussed here, four center on the "housekeeper"—*Gimme a Break!*, *Who's the Boss*, *Mr. Belvedere*, and *Charles in Charge*. And this is in addition to shows like *Silver Spoons* and *Rags to Riches* that involve housekeepers managing the household, but do not focus on them. Furthermore, perhaps in response to the 1970s being completely devoid of male household labor or to the popularity of *Benson*, which ran for seven years, well into the 1980s, the 1980s is also the decade of the male housekeeper, with shows such as *Who's the Boss*, *Mr. Belvedere*, and *Charles in Charge*, in addition to the continuation of *Benson*, where male characters are almost entirely responsible for the management of the household. Distinct from the 1970s, these male housekeepers actually perform "visible" household labor, and even in the sitcoms without housekeepers, husbands return to their wives' sides at the kitchen sink, as was common in 1950s television.

The 1980s clearly responds to the lack of men performing housework in the 1970s by depicting a great deal of male household labor, which makes an analysis of housework as maternal practice even more interesting, as many of the performers of housekeeping activities in the 1980s are not mothers, nor are they always related to the individuals benefitting from the work. As I mentioned in the first chapter, viewing housework as activities of preservation—as the ability to recognize vulnerability and the willingness to meet the demands of others in an effort to preserve life—removes the biological aspects of maternal practice. This means anyone, male or female, can engage in maternal practice—a point that becomes considerably significant with regard to 1980s television. With these ideas in mind, this chapter includes the following fifteen programs from the 1980s for analysis:

Gimme a Break! (1981–1987)
Family Ties (1982–1989)
Silver Spoons (1982–1987)
Webster (1983–1989)
The Cosby Show (1984–1992)
Who's the Boss (1984–1992)
Charles in Charge (1984–1990)
Growing Pains (1985–1992)
Mr. Belvedere (1985–1990)
Golden Girls (1985–1992)
Mama's Family (1986–1990)
Alf (1986–1990)

My Two Dads (1987–1990)
Roseanne (1988–1997)
Family Matters (1989–1998)

GIMME A BREAK! (1981–1987)

Gimme a Break! aired on NBC for six years and starred Nell Carter as Nell Harper, the housekeeper to widowed police chief Carl Kanisky (Dolph Sweet) and his three daughters, Samantha (Lara Jill Miller), Julie (Lauri Hendler), and Katie (Kari Michaelsen). *Gimme a Break!* can be understood as a combination of *The Andy Griffith Show* and *Benson*. First, Nell is serving as their housekeeper not because she needs the job, but because Carl's deceased wife asked Nell to help the family as a favor before she died. This is similar to *Benson*'s arrangement when he is asked by friends to help the Governor; yet, it reflects *The Andy Griffith Show* in that it depicts a working class family who simply can't run a household without an adult female to manage the housework. However, unlike Benson, Nell is constantly doing very active, visible housework—housework that centers her character.

Nell is a very different type of housekeeper, though, from the Mrs. Garrett, Hazel, and Alice characters that precede her, as her character does not embody the same care in her work as other similar characters. Typical housework for Nell involves brushing crumbs under the couch to hide them, breaking tables with the vacuum cleaner when they are in the way, sweeping the floor with couch cushions, and accidentally sucking up the fish-bowl contents with her vacuum cleaner. In this way, her housework is similar to Lucy's in *I Love Lucy*, but Nell's mistakes are more deliberate, and less accidental.

Nell is the first housekeeper character analyzed in this study to take an intentional half-hearted approach to her housework, doing just enough to make things "appear" clean and to make food "appear" healthy. Even with regard to her cooking, many jokes are made of her instant cooking—in fact, we are allowed to see her instant food boxes on the kitchen counter, for example, thus rendering what is typically invisible, and even perhaps embarrassing, quite visible.

In other words, her "shortcuts" are made very visible to us, depicting her character and her domestic sphere as imperfect. Incidentally, Chief Kanisky's dialogue addresses this directly in the episode "Katie the Crook," when he tells Nell that with her cooking, his "stomach needs a head start." While this aspect of her housekeeping might seem to be an outlier of the argument presented in this study—that housework is depicted on television as being loving, thus indicating an inherent strength—Nell presents a character that outwardly does not enjoy housework. At times, we get indications that it is enjoyable, as she sings while she cleans. But her lack of care in the details of her housekeeping duties indicates she does not enjoy her work. Still, she continues to keep her promise to her deceased friend, and consequently, appears to love the family in a genuine way. Even though the quality of her work is very different from that of June Cleaver, Margaret Anderson, or even housekeepers like Alice and Hazel, the inherent strength is the same, as she engages in the preservation of life—tasks she doesn't necessarily enjoy—because she is committed to keeping her promises.

Even though Nell's housekeeping is very different from similar preceding characters, some trends established previously are still present in *Gimme a Break!* First, housework is depicted as therapy for Nell, even though it is simultaneously presented as a burden. In the episode "A Good Man Is Hard to Find," Nell is rejected by a potential date, and in response, she claims to have plenty of chores to do to distract her from a broken heart. Like Edith in *All in the Family* and Ida in *Rhoda*, Nell uses housework as distraction, as something to help her through difficult situations. Second, housework also functions as the moments family members approach Nell for advice, comfort, and guidance in their personal lives, and as with other housekeepers, she always has the right answer and is always the voice of reason. Like Alice in *The Brady Bunch*, Mrs. Garrett in *Diff'rent Strokes*, and Hazel in *Hazel*, Nell provides the emotional support the family requires beyond her housekeeping activities. Unlike Benson, though, Nell is a female, so we rarely see her advice address the Chief's professional matters, thus reinforcing the implication that females belong solely to the private/domestic sphere, while males, even housekeeping males, may exist simultaneously in both male/public/professional and female/private/domestic spheres.

The show further exposes this dichotomy through the makeup of the Kanisky family. In comparing it to other shows featuring a widowed male with children who require the help of a female for household management, such as *The Andy Griffith Show*, *Mayberry R.F.D.*, and *Diff'rent Strokes*, the kids, who are mostly male in these shows, do not partake in much of the housework. However, in *Gimme a Break!* where the Kanisky family involves three children who are female, the kids regularly help out with the housework. The family frequently offers to clear the table and wash the dishes so that Nell can be alone with a date, for example. The housework removes the family from the scene for Nell's benefit, so the self-sacrificial qualities of housework are depicted in a more reciprocal model of household management in *Gimme a Break!* than has been seen in previous shows. In fact, with regard to 1950s television, a common criticism of mother's position within her family involved the lack of focus on her needs, desires, and dreams. In her work *Ladies of the Evening*, Diana Meehan discusses an episode of *The Adventures of Ozzie and Harriet*: "When Ozzie identified typical activities of each family member in one episode, Harriet was described as 'reading a magazine' in the living room. She apparently had no outside interests other than the care and concerns of her family."[3] This could be said of certain televised housekeepers as well, but Nell's personal interests—her dates, her fashion, her friendships—are depicted as being important to the family and integral to the plots.

This is a new approach to the housekeeper-family household model, and it likely has something to do with the family structure of a single father with three daughters: the females are depicted as having the ability to recognize Nell's needs and desires—something to which male characters, young and old, seem to be oblivious. This introduces an important point, though. The fact that much of the show centers on Nell's needs and desires seems to be directly related to the depictions of her housework as lacking the elements of self-sacrifice that make it successful in other models. In this way, *Gimme a Break!* implies that Nell's selfishness makes her ability to succeed within the domestic sphere impossible—a space television typically signifies as being a self-sacrificing zone for women.

FAMILY TIES (1982–1989)

Family Ties ran for seven years on NBC and depicts the Keaton family, including mother Elyse (Meredith Baxter-Birney), husband Steven (Michael Gross), son Alex (Michael J. Fox), and daughters Mallory (Justine Bateman) and Jennifer (Tina Yothers). The Keaton family is particularly interesting because it portrays a family with a mother character whose career is more prestigious and likely higher paying than her husband's. Elyse works as an architect and Steven manages a television station. This point influences the division of labor within the Keaton household, as *Family Ties* depicts Elyse working often on her architectural plans in the home, while household tasks and parenting are shared. For this reason, the family appears to take an egalitarian approach to household management. In several episodes in the first season, Elyse is up early in the morning working in the kitchen, and Steven enters, dressed and ready for work, and automatically prepares breakfast for himself and the kids. Sometimes, Elyse even continues working, while the rest of the family eats breakfast. This aspect of the show is unlike any other. In shows with similar family models, like *Growing Pains*, the working mother still performs most of the household duties, and while *The Cosby Show* involves a similar egalitarian approach to household management, we rarely see Claire work through breakfast while her family members serve themselves and eat. The contributions of *Family Ties* to representations of housework and household management are unique in this regard.

Furthermore, the children are depicted as sharing household tasks, and Steven and Elyse split parenting duties, as well. Jennifer cooks chocolate-chip eggs, for example, which the family choke down, and Mallory helps with the grocery shopping and kitchen clean-up. Alex, their only son, however, performs far fewer tasks than the daughters, indicating that some of the same trends of gendered housework are still present here. Similarly, while Steven and Elyse clearly share parenting duties, as both parents have private, important conversations with their children, this activity is gendered as well. Steven usually talks with Alex and Elyse addresses the problems of her girls. For example, in the pilot episode, when Alex wants to have dinner at a country club that is very restrictive and does not include diverse populations, Steven is the one to talk privately with Alex about his decisions, and in the episode "Summer of 82," when Alex loses his virginity, Steven tells the women to "go to a movie so the men can talk." Incidentally, when Alex reveals his loss of virginity, Steven responds, "I didn't expect you to be giving me this news in the kitchen," as he pours them both some juice. This adds to the scholarship addressing 1950s television that indicates that many of the important familial discussions, the "living room lectures," occur in the living room or study—household zones that are often identified as being more male than female. In this scene, we witness two males discussing the topic of sex over juice in the kitchen, thus representing an integration of male and female spheres.

On the other hand, in the episode "I Know Jennifer's Boyfriends," Jennifer is being teased about making friends with a boy. Elyse enters Jennifer's room to talk, and her room is a mess. Elyse asks if they can talk, and Jennifer responds, "Sure, as long as it's not about cleaning my room." This points to another unique contribution of this show. The parents are depicted as choosing their battles. Elyse expresses her desire for Jennifer to have a clean room in this scene, but she ultimately lets the point go because the emotional needs of her daughter are obviously greater at the moment. The parents are depicted as having and implementing very realistic expectations for their children and home. During this conversation between Elyse and Jennifer, Elyse explains to her daughter that it is especially important for women to be strong. Jennifer responds, "You're not going to put the pressure of the entire women's movement on me, are you?" Elyse makes the strength discussed throughout this study explicit through her dialogue, underscoring the idea that the strength of women can manifest merely by making good decisions, especially when they are difficult. She encourages Jennifer to make friends with individuals she enjoys, regardless of gender, implying this is an example of exercising strength as a woman.

Whereas the show lays bare new trends with regard to household management, it also maintains some developments from the 1950s. In the evenings, while Steven reads the paper on the couch, Elyse is almost always either repairing a couch cushion or sewing, something witnessed regularly with the televised housewives of the 1950s. And when the family sits down for more formal dinners, Elyse often excuses herself from the table to fetch food or drinks to serve, thus removing her from the scene. This is an important point, though, as *Family Ties* connects the past to the present by integrating old models of household management with new ones. Since both parents seem satisfied with their shared domestic roles, there exists simultaneously a visible, physically romantic relationship between Steven and Elyse, in addition to noticeable fulfillment with their jobs and leisure/labor ratios—qualities also unique to this show. According to Hesse-Biber and Carter, in reality, this is directly related to an egalitarian approach to housework, as they report, "Wives in households with an egalitarian division of housework report greater satisfaction than those who do all of the housework. Women who receive help with housework from their husbands are usually more satisfied with their jobs than those who do not."[4] In this way, *Family Ties* does, as Barthes claims, reflect and signify what society thinks about itself.

In committing to this egalitarian approach, Steven and Elyse are sharing the desire to preserve life, but this does not mean roles are not established. The 1950s focused on the importance of adhering to male/female-determined roles, and this contributed to an approach to parenting that involved mutual efforts. *Family Ties* also depicts roles, but these roles are flexible and fluid. Steven might be responsible for breakfast one morning because Elyse worked late, but she will be depicted completing those tasks the following morning, for example. Whereas this may seem like a common-sense approach to household management, one that reflects many of our realities presently, it is not one commonly depicted on television until the 1980s.

SILVER SPOONS (1982–1987)

Silver Spoons ran for five years on NBC and starred Ricky Schroder as Ricky Stratton, son of wealthy toy-business owner, Richard Stratton III (Joel Higgins). This show is another example of the single male head of household, and like similar shows—*Family Affair*, *Diff'rent Strokes*, and *Benson*—Richard is wealthy and performs no housework. The interesting contribution of *Silver Spoons* to this study is the depiction of a household where the housework is almost completely invisible. In the pilot episode, for example, Richard's lawyer and business manager tell him he has run out of money and is broke. He doesn't understand what this means. The lawyer says, "It means no more yacht races in Florida. It means no more weekends in Paris. It means no more servants in this house." Richard responds, "Wait just

Figure 5.1 *Silver Spoons, Season One,* **"Pilot,"** © ELP Communications Inc., Courtesy Sony Pictures Television.

a minute. I draw the line at servants!" The lawyer explains that servants get paid: "they will not work for free," he says. Richard claims, "Mine will. They've been with me since I was a child. They love me. They would never leave me." At that point, all four servants—a cook, two maids, and a butler—exit the house with their bags.

This is important because it comments upon shows like *Hazel, The Andy Griffith Show, The Brady Bunch,* and *Diff'rent Strokes* with housekeepers playing surrogate mother roles. As this study has revealed, the personal needs and desires of these housekeeper characters are rarely addressed. The characters exist for the sole purpose of serving a family that is not their own, but a family that supposedly functions *like* family. The families seek out the advice, comfort, and guidance of these housekeepers as they would from family members, especially mothers, but the housekeepers' personal needs are rarely a part of the plots. The housekeepers reflect the self-sacrificial qualities of the housewife-mother characters, as they care not just for the home, but also for life-preserving needs of the family members. Shows that involve these housekeeper-as-surrogate-mothers depict them as being completely satisfied with their situations, and viewers are left to infer that the housekeepers would choose to stay, even if the work were unwaged. The housekeepers would then function like the housewife characters, who are depicted as being fulfilled by the same housekeeper duties—duties that are, in their situations, unwaged.

Silver Spoons reveals this as a misconception regarding the loyalty of servants when housework becomes unwaged, and points toward the importance of housework functioning as preservative activity, as the servants who have cared for Richard since he was a child, leave with the threat of not being paid. This also comments upon the work of the housewife characters, who are depicted as performing housework happily and unwaged, out of love and a desire to preserve. The servants' exit in this scene in *Silver Spoons* immediately distinguishes between these characters, housewife and housekeeper, underscoring the strength of the housewife who often serves in ways that are only compensated through intangible means.

Another interesting point in this show involves the invisibility of housework. It is assumed that Richard hires back his servants, once the loss of his millions is found to be an error. We never see these housekeepers, but we assume they take care of the home because Richard and Ricky never do any visible housework, yet the house is always clean. It is interesting that housework representations are common in similar shows of the era like *Diff'rent Strokes* and *Gimme a Break!* involving single men as heads of households, but they are almost non-existent in *Silver Spoons*. This show is, however, the only show where the parent and child roles are truly reversed. (We see this temporarily between Blaire and her mother on *Facts of Life*, but once the mother takes on more domestic duties, they return to their appropriate mother/daughter functions.) Ricky is depicted from the beginning as being more mature than his father, and he even "parents" his father explicitly sometimes by telling him to be sure to eat his vegetables. The discipline of performing chores for the benefit of the household is a lesson parents often teach children. Since the parent in *Silver Spoons* is depicted as a child, the management of the household is depicted from the perspective of a child as well. In other words, to a child, housework often doesn't exist. It is, in many ways, invisible, as children do not always see the work involved in their care. This is consistent with the depiction of housework in *Silver Spoons*. The house is always clean, but nobody has to clean it—a perspective that reflects Richard's childish approach to life.

WEBSTER (1983–1989)

Webster aired for six years on ABC and in syndication. It starred Emmanuel Lewis as Webster, a young boy who loses his parents and is adopted by his godfather, George Papadapolis (Alex Karras) and his new wife Katharine

(Susan Clark). George and Katharine married impulsively, and much of the show centers on their new roles of spouses and parents. Consequently, the show says quite a bit about the nature of housework and the often gendered activities of housekeeping. It also serves as an example of the ways in which television has changed very little in signifying meaning in this regard. In the 1950s, 1960s, and 1970s, especially in shows like *Bewitched*, *I Dream of Jeannie*, and *Rhoda*, we see female characters transition from singlehood to wifehood and motherhood, and these characters always express a desire to care properly for their home and family members.

In *Webster*, Katharine, a career woman, marries George shortly after meeting him, and they are immediately faced with taking in Webster. Katharine claims throughout the first several episodes that she does "not know the first thing about being a mom or wife," implying that such roles must be learned. On the one hand, Katharine's characterization resists the misconception that housework is a natural attribute of females, but at the same time, this characterization ignores the love that *is* natural and inherent in caring for family members. Still, the show often takes Katharine's ignorance of housekeeping too far. During their first morning together, George asks Katharine to make coffee, but she doesn't know how, for example. This might be believable if Katharine had previously employed a housekeeper, but she does not. In fact, Katharine is portrayed as being successful enough in her career as a consumer advocate to own a luxurious high-rise apartment, but unlike similar male characters—those in *Family Affair*, *Diff'rent Strokes*, and *Silver Spoons*, to name a few—Katharine does not have a housekeeper. She has a male secretary, who claims to control things like decorating her apartment and such, but she does not have a housekeeper. This is consistent with the trend established by television in previous decades: single males hire housekeepers, while single females, even successful ones like Katharine, are responsible for their own housekeeping.

Katharine's attempts to become domesticated, something the show very clearly depicts as learned behavior, not natural behavior, serve as much of the comedy in the early episodes. For example, in the first episode, she wants to win Webster's trust back, after he runs away, so she tries to cook. Webster reminds her that she doesn't know how. Still, she tries and ends up burning the bacon, overfilling the waffle iron, and allowing the pot on the stove to boil over. Her cooking is depicted as messy, but Webster endearingly says she reminds him of his mom who "couldn't make steam." In another episode, she tries to teach herself to cook by watching a cooking show, but she continues to fail. She says, "I'm a wife now, and I think I should be able to do wifely things." Her dialogue implies that she expects these abilities to be natural for her, but her actions reveal they are not. Her dialogue is also interestingly similar to housewife dialogue from previous decades, like when

Samantha Stephens declares in *Bewitched*, "I'm a wife now, so no more magic," or in *Rhoda*, when Ida asks Rhoda what she made for Joe's first meal as a husband. The desire of women to serve husbands has been depicted by television fairly consistently for four decades. But *Webster* adds nuance to this because it depicts a female character who has this desire to serve but not the ability, thus conveying the message that this is *not* a natural transition for all women.

Webster often reverses activities that are gendered as male or female by other shows, likely having some connection to Katharine's professional success. For Webster's birthday, for example, George is responsible for icing the birthday cake, while Katharine takes on the task of assembling a bicycle for a gift. Typically, visual culture would place the female in the kitchen with the cake and the male with the technical task of assembling a bicycle. Also, in various scenes where Katharine is trying to learn to cook, the kitchen and meal have the appearance of success. Upon tasting her cooking, though, Katharine is the first to walk over to the phone and order take-out for the family. It is unique to have Katharine criticize her own cooking, instead of a more common husband-wife plot where the new husband chokes down the bad cooking of his new bride. In *Webster*, Katharine finds her own cooking to be terrible and immediately takes the initiative to get her family fed. That initiative is representative of what *is* natural and inherent for Katharine in caring for the home—the desire to preserve.

THE COSBY SHOW (1984–1992)

The Cosby Show ran for eight years on NBC and depicts the Huxtable family, including husband Cliff (Bill Cosby), wife Claire (Phylicia Rashad), daughters Sondra (Sabrina Le Beauf), Denise (Lisa Bonet), Vanessa (Tempestt Bledsoe), and Rudy (Keshia Knight Pulliam), and son Theo (Malcolm-Jamal Warner). This show is interesting in how the pilot episode differs egregiously from the rest of the show. In the pilot, Claire performs almost all of the cooking and cleaning, and the show initially depicts household management in a way that is similar to shows of the 1950s. Claire perpetually wears an apron and serves the family, demanding that Cliff be the one to punish Theo for his bad grades. Even though it differs slightly from the 1950s domestic sitcoms where the father would consult the wife, usually while performing housework, and then have a private discussion with the children, it reflects a wife handling the housework and the father, even at the request of the mother, handling the important discussions with the children. In this pilot episode, Claire also demands that her daughter Denise help her clear the table, again furthering certain tasks as being female and others male, and Theo's room is messy, while the girls' rooms are clean, indicating a natural desire and ability for females to create clean spaces.

This approach to household management changes drastically, though, after the pilot episode, especially with regard to Cliff's contribution to domestic labor. Cliff dons his apron and cooks quite often for the family, even going as far as teaching the children to cook. At the same time, Claire is depicted as sharing many of the important discussions with children. The Huxtables are portrayed as having the most egalitarian approach to housekeeping witnessed on television in this study so far. Nearly all tasks are portrayed as being shared equally, not just between Claire and Cliff, but also with the children. Furthermore, Cliff moves his medical practice to the home, an aspect of the show that echoes Alex Stone in *The Donna Reed Show* from the 1950s—and also something that becomes a trend in the 1980s with shows like *Growing Pains*. In discussing the favorable hours of father characters in the 1950s, and Alex Stone's in-home medical practice, Leibman argues that "Because of their remarkable proximity, the fathers are made privy to all of their children's dilemmas and delights, usurping mother's traditional position as the in-home boss." This is somewhat true of *The Cosby Show*, but Claire has a career also as a successful attorney. She is depicted as desiring a parenting relationship that is shared. Still, Cliff's in-home practice does center him and his housekeeping activities in the show, with Claire often entering the home asking, "What's for dinner?" This is not to say that Claire doesn't contribute to the household management, as she is often seen performing housekeeping duties. *The Cosby Show*'s contribution to housework analyses is important because it provides a very popular example of a male who is comfortable and confident performing tasks of preservation within his domestic sphere, and it is one of the earliest televised examples of the ways in which activities of "maternal practice" can be performed by males or females.

WHO'S THE BOSS (1984–1992)

Who's the Boss aired for eight years on ABC and starred Tony Danza as Tony Micelli, a retired baseball player who takes a job as a live-in housekeeper for a family, in an effort to give his daughter, Samantha (Alyssa Milano), a better home and school. He is hired by a divorced, successful career woman, Angela Bower (Judith Light), and her son Jonathan (Danny Pintauro). Tony is the fourth male housekeeper included in this study, after Bub on *My Three Sons*, Mr. French on *Family Affair*, and Benson on *Soap* and *Benson*, and other than Benson's occasional duties on *Soap*, he is the first to be actively and visibly engaged in housework. Any "feminizing" this activity may have on his character is balanced by his former role as a professional baseball player. The obvious conclusion is that television in the 1980s believes it is more acceptable for a man—one who is not working to preserve the lives of his family members—to do housework when he is presented as a hyper-masculinized professional athlete. Tony performs all of the cooking and cleaning for a successful business woman and her family, and this depiction not only is a response to the complete void of male domestic labor in the 1970s, but also functions to break the chain of shows depicting wealthy single males with housekeepers and single females without domestic help.

Traditional roles are reversed in *Who's the Boss*, as Tony is depicted as being concerned with cleanliness and healthy cooking, while Angela is portrayed as being very messy. In the first episodes, Tony doesn't feel comfortable cleaning her bedroom or bathroom because he regards it as too personal, too private. The first time we see Angela's room, it is a mess. When they address the issue of laundry, he claims to feel uncomfortable cleaning her "skimpies." She tells him this is part of the job, and shows him where to put away her panties, hose, and bras. He is clearly uneasy with this, and it is the first example of housework being used to indicate intimacy. Tony believes washing certain clothing items signifies an inappropriate closeness with his employer. This is interesting because Hazel, Aunt Bee, Alice, and Mrs. Garrett, all female housekeepers serving males, are never depicted as feeling uncomfortable with these tasks, and they also never set housekeeping boundaries, as Bub does when he will not fold laundry or as Tony does when he will not wash undergarments. The hyper-masculinized Tony and his relationship with a successful female employer is immediately sexualized, underscoring the notion that it is "okay" for women to clean the underwear of men but inappropriate for men to clean the underwear of women. It also highlights the self-sacrificial qualities of women performing housework in visual culture, as has been discussed previously. Perhaps the willingness of females to self-sacrifice is the reason they are not depicted as being conflicted over washing a male's "skimpies," versus the self-serving qualities of the male housekeeper who exposes the sexuality of the situation. This is similar to Benson refusing to cook anything he himself will not eat.

Traditional role expectations and reversals are made explicit through dialogue. When Angela's mother wants her to hire Tony as the housekeeper, Angela resists it because he is male. The mother says, "Don't be sexist. A man can do meaningless, unproductive work just as well as a woman!" Like the character Katharine in *Webster*, Angela admits, "I may not be great in the kitchen, but I certainly make up for it in the board room." Unfortunately, also like the show *Webster*, *Who's the Boss* implies that a woman can only be good at one or the other—her career or domesticity. Angela has chosen career, so the show states directly that Angela can't cook.

Figure 5.2 *Who's the Boss? Season One,* "Pilot," © ELP Communications Inc., Courtesy Sony Pictures Television.

While the show initially tries to feminize Tony as a housekeeper, calling him a "male Mary Poppins" in the dialogue, he is soon hyper-masculinized, as he is the first televised housekeeper in this study to work out while he cleans house. When he needs to vacuum under the couch, for example, he pumps the couch up and down like a set of weights.

He uses housework as an opportunity to increase muscle mass and intensify his masculinity. This works to combat any feminizing that has occurred through Angela's doubts in hiring a male housekeeper or through the dialogue.

Even though they do not engage in an official relationship, the flirtatious interactions between Tony and Angela are unique to housekeeper-employer models on television, and this indicates another way television admits an awkwardness with a male housekeeper working for a successful female. George never flirts with Hazel in *Hazel*, Mike is never attracted to Alice in *The Brady Bunch*, and Mr. Drummond has no awkward feelings for Mrs. Garrett in *Diff'rent Strokes*, for example. Tony does use housework as a distraction, though, as these other housekeeper characters do, when he does not want to deal with the awkwardness of their attraction for each other. If Angela attempts to discuss the attraction with him, he turns to dusting or vacuuming as distractions, something that connects his housework to that of previous shows. Most important, *Who's the Boss* not only serves as the first example of a hyper-masculinized male character serving a successful woman, but also as the first example of sexualized housework, thus indicating television's discomfort with these traditional role reversals.

CHARLES IN CHARGE (1984–1990)

Charles in Charge aired for six years on CBS and in syndication and starred Scott Baio as Charles, a college student who serves as housekeeper and baby-sitter to the Pembroke family[5] in exchange for room and board. Charles is another example of a male housekeeper in the 1980s who actively performs housework and parenting—another sure response to the lack of male domestic labor in the 1970s—but his character differs from Tony Micelli in *Who's the Boss* because Charles is employed by a married couple and their children, a situation which serves to remove the potential for romantic relationships between employer and employee.

Charles is more than just a housekeeper, though. Even though previous similar household models have depicted family members as seeking advice and guidance from housekeepers, as with Hazel, Alice, and Mrs. Garrett, the Pembroke parents give Charles almost exclusive parenting rights. Charles will regularly prepare the children's meals and clean up after them, like other televised housekeepers, but when the kids have actual problems in life that need to be addressed, Charles will defer to the parents—a response that is also similar to other housekeeper characters. However, in this show, the parents tell Charles, "Just handle it. That's what we pay you for." In other words, *Charles in Charge* depicts an arrangement where the housekeeper's emotional involvement in their lives is not just a happenstance byproduct of the time he spends with them, but something that can be purchased for a wage. This model of household management goes beyond what we have seen previously, even in programs depicting family-like relationships between housekeeper and employer. Charles's love and concern for the children are depicted as being purchased, something that distinguishes his housekeeping duties from similar female characters, whose love and concern are portrayed as occurring naturally.

GROWING PAINS (1985–1992)

Growing Pains ran for seven years on ABC and depicts the Seaver family, including wife Maggie (Joanna Kerns), husband Jason (Alan Thicke), daughters Carol (Tracey Gold) and Chrissy (Ashley Johnson), and sons Mike (Kirk Cameron) and Ben (Jeremy Miller). After being home with the kids, Maggie decides to return to work as a reporter, and Jason has his psychiatric practice in the home, following a model similar to *The Donna Reed Show* and *The Cosby Show*. This situation makes Jason's proximity to the home and family very close, but the show depicts Maggie doing most of the housework and Jason handling most of the important conversations with the children, echoing the critical analyses of 1950s television shows such as *Leave It to Beaver* and *Father Knows Best*. The show's intro even indicates its connection to the past, as it includes historical photos of various families. One possible indication of this intro is that the show is positioning itself—its familial model of "stay-at-home" father and working mother—within this historical context that reveals several "types" of families. Interestingly, though, the Seavers are not very different, even though their claims may say otherwise. In the first episode, which is similar to the rest of the first season, it is Maggie's first day back to work. She cooks breakfast while Jason sits down to read the paper. She sends the kids off to school and clears the breakfast table. She does all of this before Jason even gets dressed for work. While this is just one episode in a season, the show seems to regress by implying that Maggie not only got herself dressed and ready for work, she got the children and their lunches ready for school, and she fixed the family breakfast before Jason even awakened. When he does awaken, he kisses his wife, sits down at the table, reads the paper while eating breakfast, and then leisurely begins to get ready for the day. Instead of highlighting mother's new role in the workforce, the episode functions to underscore dad's laziness.

Later in the episode, when Mike has a problem, he seeks out Jason for help. Even in the programs of the 1950s, sons are depicted as approaching mothers for emotional support more often than in *Growing Pains*, which is surprising considering its "modern" familial model of working mother and stay-at-home father. Although Jason is seen assuming additional smaller tasks in later episodes, Maggie still functions to perform the majority of the housework, and Jason serves the emotional needs of the children. Within this study, I can find no other show that makes a stronger return to 1950s televised family models. However, by depicting the "double duty" nature of Maggie's day so egregiously, the show underscores the robust qualities of her character.

MR. BELVEDERE (1985–1990)

Mr. Belvedere aired for five years on ABC and portrays the English male housekeeper, Lynn Belvedere (Christopher Hewitt), and the family he serves, the Owens, including husband George (Bob Uecker), wife Marsha

(Ilene Graff), sons Kevin (Rob Stone) and Wesley (Brice Beckham), and daughter Heather (Tracy Wells). Mr. Belvedere responds to a request by the Owens for a housekeeper, and their need for domestic help is established in the first episode. George works and Marsha has gone back to school, so the pilot episode depicts the kids alone at home, responsible for cooking dinner. Heather, specifically, has been told by her mother to cook dinner if the parents don't make it home in time. Kevin is older than Heather, yet because Heather is their only daughter, she is made responsible for cooking dinner. Also, the mother has made the casserole ahead of time, so that the kids merely have to put it in the oven. Heather is on the phone, so she tells Kevin to do it, and Wesley reveals that Kevin nearly started a fire the last time he used a kitchen appliance. The show depicts the Owens family as subscribing to the ideology that because Heather is female, she is naturally capable of using the kitchen, versus Kevin, who is incapable because he is male. When the mother gets home, she chides Heather for being on the phone and not cooking dinner, even though all three children are present in the kitchen and not doing anything. This is important because the show is establishing how gendered the family's perceptions of housework are—a plot point that becomes significant when the domestic agency sends them a male housekeeper.

The dialogue furthers the family's need for domestic help, as Marsha tells the kids to be patient because they are seeking help from a domestic agency, and the house is portrayed as a mess, with clothes all over the living room. Mr. Belvedere arrives wearing a suit, and Marsha immediately believes he will not fit their needs because he is male, even though he presents her with reference letters from previous employers, including Winston Churchill. She says, "Do you know *anything* about cooking?" When he answers in the affirmative, she tells him their needs go beyond cooking to include cleaning and parenting—all things Marsha assumes he can't do because he is male. She tells him to have a seat on the couch and asks if she can get him anything. He pulls out a handful of popcorn from the couch cushions, saying, "No, this popcorn will be plenty." Ultimately, George and Marsha decide he will not suffice as their housekeeper, but they allow him to stay overnight. He prepares and serves them breakfast in the morning, convincing them of his abilities, and the family allows him to stay.

Mr. Belvedere is interesting for several reasons. First, the Owens family is depicted as having strict ideals for male and female domestic duties. This is made clear both through Marsha, who is in law school full-time but is still responsible for the housekeeping duties (much like Maggie in *Growing Pains*), along with her daughter Heather, and also through the family's explicit reservations regarding a male housekeeper's domestic abilities. Whereas the show underscores the fallacy of the Owens' gendered misconceptions of housework and housekeepers, considering Mr. Belvedere is male *and* is extraordinarily skilled in the performance of domestic duties, the show, at the same time, feminizes Mr. Belvedere, implying that he is this good because he has feminine qualities, an aspect of the show that echoes Bub's character in *My Three Sons*. Much of this occurs through Mr. Belvedere's conflicts with the patriarchal character George.

George is depicted as having an extreme love of sports, as he is not only employed as a sports writer, he plays football and attends wrestling events with his boys—all plot points used to highlight George's masculinity. Mr. Belvedere is portrayed, through some of visual culture's typical indicators, as having more feminine qualities, as he dances around the kitchen while cooking, and has a love and appreciation of ballet and classical music. His interests often conflict with George's interests, especially when Mr. Belvedere influences the children's interests, and this creates much of the comedy of the show. *Mr. Belvedere*'s male housekeeper character stands in opposition to Tony in *Who's the Boss*, which ran simultaneously, but the depictions actually signify similar meanings. *Mr. Belvedere* depicts a feminized male who is extraordinary at housework, while *Who's the Boss* portrays a hyper-masculinized male, who is initially terrible at housework. While the depictions are different, the signified messages, although fallacies, are the same: men are not naturally suited to function within their domestic spheres and women are, and when a man takes on domestic duties and is automatically successful, he is depicted as also taking on feminine qualities. Within the context of this study, it seems television is indicating, especially through drastically different portrayals of male and female housekeepers, that the female desire and drive to preserve life, to meet the demands of others, is stronger than it is in males.

GOLDEN GIRLS (1985–1992)

Golden Girls aired for seven years on NBC and depicts four mature, widowed or divorced women sharing a house in Miami, Florida. Characters include Dorothy Zbornak (Beatrice Arthur), Blanche Devereaux (Rue McClanahan), Rose Nylund (Betty White), and Sophia Petrillo (Estelle Getty). Throughout the series, the four women share all aspects of housekeeping. However, in the pilot episode, the women have a male housekeeper named Coco (Charles Levin). They refer to him as their "gay cook," as Rose says. Like Mr. Belevedere, the male housekeeper is feminized, and their interactions with this aspect of his characterization constitute some of the show's comedy in this episode. Sophia initially refers to him as the "fancy man in the kitchen," and then later when they plan to go to the dog races together, she says, "He's an okay petunia." Blanche apologizes for these offensive comments by claiming Sophia's "stroke censored her brain." This character is eliminated, however, after the pilot episode, and the four women become responsible for all housekeeping duties.

Even though the male housekeeper character disappears after the first episode, the first season involves some interesting dialogue regarding the lives and work of women as mothers and wives. In the same episode, Blanche's fiancé does not show up for their wedding because he has been arrested for bigamy. Distraught and feeling desperate about this being her "last chance" to get married again, Blanche says to Dorothy, "The kids leave and our husbands die. Is that some kind of test? We are alone, Dorothy. What do we do?" Similarly, in the episode "Guess Who's Coming to the Wedding," Dorothy confronts her ex-husband Stan (Herbert Edelman) about walking out on her without telling her he was leaving her. She says, "We had thirty-eight years together of sharing, of loving, of crying, of school plays and little league." Her dialogue makes explicit the value women place on their housekeeping and parenting activities. This early dialogue also reflects their individual transitions, some depicted as being more difficult than others, from serving others—from being needed by others earlier in their lives—to having to serve themselves and eventually each other later in life. In this way, the dialogue implies that women possess a natural need to serve and a need for their services to be needed. Ultimately, though, *Golden Girls* depicts these four friends as finding fulfillment through serving themselves and each other— another unique model of household management.

These transitions and the subsequent individual lessons learned regarding the roles of women are an important part of the show as well. In the same "Wedding" episode, Dorothy's daughter is getting married. Dorothy tells her, "Be a good wife. Be his friend. Be his lover. But don't be his slave." This is the advice of a mother who has, presumably, filled all of these roles at some point in her life, as she is able to tell her daughter which roles will fulfill her and which ones won't. Certainly, television in every decade has depicted women in various forms and on various levels as wives, friends, lovers, and slaves to their spouses. Dorothy's explicit advice to her daughter acknowledges the multitude of roles women fill, some more meaningful than others.

Housework functions as comedy and as moments for female bonding. When a character is having a problem, it is typical to see others serve her food or drink, while they all talk. In these moments, the women serve, share, bond, and consequently, laugh. In the episode, "Rose the Prude," for example, Rose is the one with an issue, so everyone gathers around the table over coffee to discuss. Blanche goes to the refrigerator to get cream, and Sophia warns her as she selects a container, "Watch what you're grabbing. I've got a specimen in there." In this way, television integrates housework and comedy with ageism, a common plot device in the series.

Even though the women appear to share housework equally, as the owner of the home, Blanche wears an apron more often than her roommates in the first season. She also uses the cleanliness of her house to compete with others, as she claims to "have cleaned the house from top to bottom" to impress her sister, for example. The four women perform housekeeping tasks together, but Blanche's apron often designates her iconographically as the one most responsible for these duties—a point furthered also by her ownership of the home, thus positioning her as the "landlord." Whereas this point may seem surprising, considering that the overly-sexualized Blanche is also depicted as the most self-serving of the four women, her explicit housework is often being performing to impress or compete.

Most important, though, *Golden Girls* furthers the trend that single women, whether young, professional, or in this case elderly and divorced or widowed, are responsible for their own housework, while single men, whether young, professional, or divorced/widowed, almost always have a housekeeper character to perform these duties for them. Even when the characters are older, as they are in *Golden Girls*, television signifies single females as being capable and determined at any age to preserve life—a point that is underscored by the removal of the male housekeeper, Coco, in this series after the pilot episode.

MAMA'S FAMILY (1986–1990)

Mama's Family ran for four years on NBC and starred Vicki Lawrence as matriarch Thelma Harper, who is depicted as cooking and cleaning for her mostly ungrateful family and nonfamily members. The show's contribution to this study involves Thelma's attitude while performing housework, which is less than cheerful. There appears to be a bitterness to her housework, which is something that has not been common to females performing housework in previous shows. In fact, depictions have reflected just the opposite—females who are so fulfilled by domestic work that they often sing and dance while they work. When the children visit Thelma, they expect her to cook their meals and do their laundry, and her frustration with housework comes not from the actual activities, but from their expectations that she will perform them without assistance or gratitude.

Mama's Family exposes directly the idea that a significant aspect of the fulfillment of housework on television is the realization that others are benefitting from the labor. I am not claiming that all previous characters have been explicitly thanked for their housework, but television usually portrays the individuals being served as being better individuals because of the housekeeping contributions. Thelma does not have this experience with those she serves, as they seem to become increasingly ill-mannered. *Mama's Family* implies that a requirement for fulfilling housework involves knowing the work sustains and even improves life. When this aspect is removed from housework activities, they are depicted as drudgery.

ALF (1986–1990)

Alf ran for four years on NBC and involves an Alien Life Form (ALF) crash landing in the Tanner's garage. Alf's home planet has exploded, so the Tanner family takes him in as a family member. Characters include father Willie (Max Wright), wife Kate (Anne Schedeen), daughter Lynn (Andrea Elson), and son Brian (Benji Gregory). The premise of *Alf* echoes the trend in the 1960s to create shows depicting the supernatural and fantastic, as Alf is an extraterrestrial family member in the Tanner household. He is established as feeling "at home" with them in the second episode, when he dons an apron and oven mitt, and begins cooking in the kitchen. Housework is used to establish Alf's position as an accepted member of the family. It is also used, however, to distinguish Alf from the other characters. In the same scene, Alf decides to make a peanut butter and jelly sandwich, and Kate asks him not to get his hair in the peanut butter. He later asks, "Did you say I should or should not get hair in the peanut butter," indicating he did exactly what Kate asked him not to do. He proceeds to accidentally set the kitchen on fire. Later in this episode, the family is seated around the table eating dinner, when they encounter Alf's hairs in their tuna. Whereas housework is used to integrate Alf into the home and family, it also functions to separate him as "the other."

Housework is gendered in *Alf*, as other than Alf's momentary domestic duties in the early episodes, Kate and her daughter Lynn handle almost all the cleaning and cooking for the family. The only other character who really performs housework is another female, Kate's mother. When the mother visits, she wears an apron and carries a handheld vacuum cleaner, and her arguments with Kate frequently center on her disapproval of Kate's housework choices, such as the type of floor cleaner she uses. Even though Alf is initially presented as performing housework—a depiction that explicitly ties him to the Tanner domestic sphere—his kitchen mistakes place him with the other males in the show, in roles that avoid domestic labor.

MY TWO DADS (1987–1990)

My Two Dads aired for three years on NBC and starred Staci Keanan as Nicole Bradford, a twelve-year-old girl whose mother dies. The mother leaves custody of Staci to two men she dated earlier in her life, financial executive Michael Taylor (Paul Reiser) and artist Joey Harris (Greg Evigan). The show depicts two single men raising a daughter, and considering this is a unique household model, some points are worth making regarding their housework. First, the character Joey represents the third character in this decade that functions as an adult male child. This is also true of Richard Stratton in *Silver Spoons* and Vinton Harper in *Mama's Family*. These male characters are depicted as "doofus dads," who can barely take care of themselves, much less their children—a trend exemplified in concurrent advertising, as well. As a third example, Joey establishes this characterization as a trend in television. In the first episode, when Joey brings Nicole to his apartment for the first time, she asks for lunch. He gives her several take-out options, and she responds, "How about tuna fish here?" Joey doesn't understand because all he has to eat or drink in his house is champagne. This is very similar to Richard Stratton and his son Ricky in *Silver Spoons*. Even though Ricky is the child, he is depicted as parenting the adult by reminding him to eat his vegetables. Nicole has a similar function with Joey. When she opens his freezer, she finds only toys. Joey finally decides to order pizza. Once they receive the pizza, Joey and Michael are arguing over Nicole. Meanwhile, Nicole gathers plates, napkins, and silverware, and proceeds to set the table to eat. She says, "Look guys, our first meal together." Joey's domestic sphere, even though having the appearance of neatness, is depicted as having no housework performed until Nicole, a twelve-year-old female, arrives and teaches her new dads how to function in the domestic realm. Her housework also functions to bring peace and order to a situation in flux.

Another interesting contribution of this show involves the ways in which housework, as it does in *Alf*, creates and establishes home regardless of the location of the actual housing structure. In the first few episodes, Joey and Michael continue fighting over where Nicole will live, as each man wants her in his apartment. For a while, the "family" go back and forth between Joey's artistic loft and Michael's uptown traditional apartment. However, in both places, while the men further their competition with each other and their disputes over Nicole, she uses housework, usually setting tables, to establish homes in both spaces. In this way, housework is used to establish home and bring peace to confrontational situations.

At the same time, like *Alf*, housework is depicted as being a natural female attribute in *My Two Dads*, as Nicole is portrayed as teaching her new adult dads how to perform basic housekeeping tasks that they surely performed themselves prior to her arrival. Once a female penetrates the domestic spheres of the single males, housework becomes a visibly active part of those realms. Even so, this show is unique in its depiction of successful single males without housekeepers. Michael's apartment complex handles the cleaning of his apartment, but the men are not depicted as having personal housekeepers, something that has been common to previous successful single male characters in television. Nicole fills this role, once her character enters their lives.

ROSEANNE (1988–1997)

Roseanne ran for nine years on ABC and starred Roseanne Barr as matriarch Roseanne Conner. Other family members include her husband Dan (John Goodman), daughters Becky (Lecy Goranson) and Darlene (Sara Gilbert), son D.J. (Michael Fishman), and sister Jackie Harris (Laurie Metcalf). The Conners are a working-class family, with Roseanne working full-time and Dan often unemployed. *Roseanne* presents a new depiction of the mother as a no-nonsense matriarch, and the cover of the series DVD reads, "Who doesn't love a domestic goddess?" This is comedic, as Roseanne's blunt and often ill-mannered approach to housekeeping redefines "domestic goddess," especially when compared to "domestic goddess" characters from the 1950s and 1960s, such as June Cleaver, Margaret Anderson, and Samantha Stephens. First, the intro to *Roseanne* involves the viewer circling around to view every member of the family seated at the dinner table, perhaps suggesting the signification of equality in the family. The Conner house is cluttered and messy, but this doesn't function as a plot point, as it does in signifying the need for a housekeeper in shows like *Mr. Belvedere*. The Conner house is always messy because the parents are working-class individuals with very little time for domestic labor. The house reflects this lack of time and resources. But what is most unique about Roseanne is her treatment of family members. Similar to Thelma in *Mama's Family*, Roseanne does not sugar coat her statements. For example, in the first episode, when D.J. asks what's for dinner, Roseanne tells him meatloaf. He says, "You hate meatloaf." She replies, "I ain't eatin' it." When Dan enters the kitchen, she asks if he wants a beer. When he says, "sure," she tells him to get one. And when the kids are in the kitchen trying to help with small tasks, Roseanne states, "Honey, get away from here and give me all that stuff."

Roseanne is direct and blunt, which might initially be perceived as unloving—a departure from previous mother characterizations. However, nothing could be further from the truth in Roseanne's depiction. Dan is often unemployed and looking for work, and Roseanne even indicates through dialogue that when he is out of work, all he does is sit on the couch all week. The house is always a mess, but Dan is home all day. This means that Roseanne, much like the housewife characters of previous decades, is almost exclusively responsible for the housekeeping duties of her home, even though, unlike previous mother-character depictions, she is the only member of the family who is perpetually employed full-time. Her commitment to the preservation of her family, despite her long work hours, represents a level of strength and self-sacrifice that I would argue exceeds that of many similar characters, even though on the surface, Roseanne often appears unloving and harsh.

Roseanne fills both roles that are more often shared by parents in other televised depictions. She handles the housekeeping and the "living room lectures," the term coined by Leibman with regard to 1950s television. Consequently, the house is messy and their lives are depicted as being muddled as well. For example, in the episode "Language Lessons," D.J. is enjoying breakfast by eating cereal directly from the box. Roseanne eventually comes down the stairs carrying a laundry basket, when she notices D.J. has been wearing the same socks all week. She sits and loves on her son for a moment and then simply adds his socks to her laundry without a fuss. In the same scene, Darlene asks D.J. to clear off the coffee table, so he just takes one swipe, knocking all contents onto the floor. Roseanne sees this, but does not mind because she is too busy starting the laundry. She tells Dan to start making his famous four-star chili, but while he chops onions, Roseanne folds laundry on the kitchen table. Roseanne and Dan use situations such as this to show the playfulness of their relationship through housework, as she will toss laundry at him while he threatens to fling chili on her. In this way, housework signifies friendship between them, something that is also unique to this show.

Other family members perform housework as well, perhaps echoing the "equality" signified through the circular motion in the intro—equality that I can't necessarily find between Roseanne and Dan with regard to household management. Roseanne's sister Jackie comes over almost daily to do laundry, and in the aforementioned episode, when she tells Dan his chili needs salt, he replies, "You can insult my wife, and you can insult my children. But don't bad mouth my chili." Even though his dialogue here indicates concern for the quality of his cooking, Dan is depicted as performing very little life-preserving activities, especially considering his dialogue regularly indicates how he has been unemployed for weeks and is "going crazy" just sitting around the house. Even in these moments, Roseanne consoles him and provides emotional support, instead of reminding him of all the housekeeping duties that visibly need to be completed. The children, especially the oldest daughter Becky, will also contribute to the housework. Becky folds laundry and says, "Here, mom, I folded the clothes." Her dialogue indicates this task as belonging to mom, even though the children often assist. *Roseanne* depicts a mother character who, on the surface, appears blunt, harsh, ill-mannered, and at times, unloving, but her determination to preserve life and endless emotional support for family members, considering she works full-time and receives little help at home, indicates a superior strength in the mother character that is unique to this show.

FAMILY MATTERS (1989–1998)

Family Matters ran for nine years on ABC and then CBS and depicts the middle-class, African-American Winslow family of mother Harriette (JoMarie Payton), father Carl (Reginald VelJohnson), son Eddie (Darius McCrary), daughters Laura (Kellie Shanygne Williams) and Judy (Jaimee Foxworth), grandmother Estelle "Mother Winslow" (Rosetta LeNoire), aunt Rachel Crawford (Telma Hopkins), and her baby Richie (Bryton James). This show's contribution to this study is significant, as it depicts more visible housework than most shows from any decade in this study. Moreover, Harriette works full-time, has the same education as her husband, yet is employed in a far less-paying job, and she and the children perform all of the housekeeping duties. This show is reflective of 1970s shows, as the patriarch, Carl, is rarely seen performing any domestic labor, and instead is regularly portrayed napping or reading the paper on the couch while Harriette cooks dinner and the kids set the table. Even the introduction to the show includes images of Carl failing at housework, as he clumsily tries to put out a fire in the kitchen toaster and accidentally breaks a kitchen window. Mother Winslow and Aunt Rachel also perform a great deal of housework, but considering they do not work full-time, it is surprising that Harriette alone still handles the majority of the work. In fact, when Mother Winslow helps out by folding laundry or cooking dinner, Harriette thanks her for doing the work for her—clearly indicating that Harriette regards this work as her duty exclusively.

Several episodes are worth mentioning from the first season, but one deserves emphasis. In the episode "The Two-Income Family," Harriette's roles as full-time employee, full-time mom, and full-time housekeeper are addressed explicitly. Harriette graduated from the Police Academy alongside Carl, but she soon became pregnant and quit to stay home with the children. When she returned to the workforce, she claims she expected to make as much money as previously, but nobody wanted to hire her. She had to take what she could get, so she has been employed as an elevator operator at the *Chicago Chronicle* for years. This plot point references the wage gap and discrimination in the workforce directly. Carl is concerned about not being able to pay bills, so he encourages her to go to her supervisor and ask for a raise. When she does, the company lays her off, claiming they are switching to self-service elevators. Harriette spends most of the episode unsuccessfully searching for work. In the meantime, Mother Winslow assumes many of Harriette's household duties, and she cooks dinners that cost "only four dollars" to make.

She claims this expertise is a result of living through the Depression. It points to how Mother Winslow's self-worth, like so many other mother characters, is depicted as being tied directly to her housekeeping and thrift expertise. When Harriette decides to apply for a job with the *Chronicle* that requires managerial experience, she is initially rejected in the interview for lacking the requisite experience. She disagrees, however, with the interviewer, saying, "I've got managerial experience coming out of my ears. I worked here full time, and I was a full time mom. I managed a home, a household budget, and a family. And Mr. Seeger, I'm talking about a job you can't call in sick for; you can't get a raise or overtime; and you can't take a vacation. Every day, I'm a leader, an organizer, and a mediator. Those are my qualifications, and if you want references, call Eddie, Judy, and Laura Winslow and ask them about my work." After she gets home and learns she got the job, she thanks her family members for "pitching in and running the house together" for her. She then thanks Carl for encouraging her to pursue the job. This is important because Harriette's character distinguishes between the support of the husband and the support of the rest of the family. Harriette makes explicit the gendered division of labor within their home, that the patriarch is responsible for emotional support, while the females and children are responsible for "running the house." This occurs in other episodes as well, such as "Short Story," for example, when Carl asks the family who left the sprinkler on in the yard and Mother Winslow responds, "Don't look at me. I don't do outside work."

Whereas these gendered distinctions exist with regard to the adults, Harriette's character makes clear that these distinctions do not exist for the children. In the episode "Body Damage," everyone has finished eating dinner. Harriette needs to get to a PTA meeting, so she says, "I made dinner. You kids take care of the dishes." Eddie claims she must have meant the two girls, but Harriette responds, "I meant all of you." In other scenes, Harriette is cooking, while all of the children set the table, and Carl reads a magazine on the couch. One point worth mentioning regarding how visible all of this housework is in *Family Matters* involves the set. Most scenes occur within the joined kitchen and dining room space, which also houses the laundry room and a play space for the kids. In this way, the mise-en-scène contributes in a unique way to housework depictions in the Winslow household.

With regard to parenting, *Family Matters* furthers certain trends established in the 1950s, but introduces new ones as well. First, when the kids have problems, they typically go to Carl, especially when they need to buy things. Also, Carl will more often have the important discussions with the kids. For example, in the episode "Short Story," Eddie enters the kitchen looking as though he has been in a fight. Carl removes him from the kitchen where Harriette is cooking by saying, "Son, let's have a serious discussion about girls." However, in a way that is similar to *Silver Spoons*, the children do a great deal of "parenting" in *Family Matters*. In the same episode, when Harriette and Aunt Rachel are fighting, the children advise the adults to reconcile, claiming family is too important to let disagreements tear them apart. Similarly, in the episode "Body Damage," Harriette and Aunt Rachel wreck Carl's police car, and instead of admitting it to him, the adults convince the kids to hide their secret for them. The children often function as the voices of reason, while the adults make poor decisions.

It seems particularly interesting that at the end of the 1980s, two of the most popular television programs, *Family Matters* and *Roseanne*, depict full-time, employed mothers, who also handle the housekeeping exclusively. These programs return to household management models reflective of the 1950s, but they add to mother's duties by introducing full-time employment, which certainly isn't common in the 1950s. This is surprising considering the popularity of 1980s examples of *The Cosby Show* and *Family Ties*, depicting working women who have egalitarian situations at home. Because of the popularity of these shows, the inequality depicted by *Roseanne* and *Family Matters* is underscored.

CONCLUSION

Television in the 1980s certainly reflects a return to traditional family models, but even within programs like *Alf* and *My Two Dads*, depicting less-than-traditional familial models, it still revisits the focus on family in general. This is particularly evident in the trend established in this decade to use family photographs of the past and present in the intros of many of these shows. *Webster*, *The Cosby Show*, *Mr. Belvedere*, *Growing Pains*, and *Family Ties* all use show intros that depict family photographs. These photographs are typically presented in chronological order, with the oldest photos preceding photos of the present. Even the shows *Alf* and *My Two Dads* include intros reflecting the photographic image. In *Alf*, we see home video footage of the family, and in *My Two Dads*, Nicole enters the photographic worlds of her fathers, as she stares at framed photos of each of them. Considering seven of the most popular shows of the 1980s use the photographic image in some capacity to introduce these programs, it is worth deconstructing the iconography of these introductions.

It seems the introductions in the 1980s are making a point to connect the present to the past, something that parallels the return of 1980s television to traditional family shows reflective of models of the 1950s. The introductions for *Webster*, *The Cosby Show*, *Mr. Belvedere*, and *Family Ties* depict photographs of the family members as individuals, typically beginning with the husband and wife coming together or the housekeeper making his way to America, and then finishing with photographs of the individuals forming a family together. The *Growing Pains* introduction depicts images, mostly reliefs, paintings, drawings, and photographs, of various "families" from the Egyptian era, to the Renaissance, to the present, implying that even though the outward appearances of families—and visual culture's depiction of families—have changed drastically over history, the family unit in the present shares the same foundational quality of love as the family units of the past. *Growing Pains* includes a stay-at-home mom returning to work, thus adding a new twist to the housewife models of the 1950s, and this is reflected in the *Growing Pains* intro, connecting the Seavers to historical families, in a way that claims, "We're not so different after all."

In addition to the idea that the iconography of photographs connects the family in the present to the family of the past, it is also self-reflexive—it recognizes itself as photographic images through depictions of photographic images and consequently highlights the importance of the photographic image. Just as Barthes connects the signified image to what society thinks of itself and Hall claims we make meaning in these images, the use of photographs in these introductions acknowledges the significance of images in establishing meaning regarding our society, our cultures, our relationships, our families, and our lives. In *Alf*, for example, the introduction involves Alf walking around the house, filming family members in unexpected ways, invading their most private moments. He catches the mother getting out of the shower, and he finds the daughter hiding in a closet talking on the phone. Alf uses photography to invade their privacy in the same way that television penetrates the domestic sphere. The iconography of the photographic image, in this case video, functions to reveal the premise of the show, which involves Alf crash landing into their lives and becoming a part of the family because there is no other option for him. Similarly, in other shows like *Webster*, *Family Ties*, and *The Cosby Show*, the introductions force us to acknowledge the significance of images, as it is the only way we are allowed to access the pasts of these televised families, and consequently, television sends the message that we need to understand the past in order to appreciate the present.

This is important because in the 1980s, television presents many new approaches to household management, but the common iconography of these introductions, in addition to a few identifiable trends, connects these families not just to each other but also to the long history of television families. In this decade, male characters perform more housework, as we find not just egalitarian marriages like the Keatons on *Family Ties* and the Huxtables on *The Cosby Show*, but also hyper-masculinized male housekeepers, as in *Who's the Boss* and feminized male housekeeper characters, as in *Mr. Belvedere* and *Golden Girls*. We also find career-driven *and* nurturing female characters, such as Katharine in *Webster* and Angela in *Who's the Boss*, who reveal that housekeeping is not a natural female attribute and dispel an idea laid bare in the 1950s that career-driven women need to be reformed, as they will find ultimate fulfillment through housewifery. The 1980s presents female characters who find fulfillment through both careers and homemaking simultaneously, even if the female characters struggle initially to develop certain housekeeping skills. But the common iconography of these shows claims that even though the 1980s presents so many different depictions of household management, some things remain the same—qualities that are common to all of our television families. This study argues that this commonality is the desire to preserve life, by recognizing and meeting the demands of others, especially loved ones, through housekeeping tasks, and the subsequent fulfillment found in seeing others benefit from this important work.

NOTES

1. Marc, *Comic Visions*, 217.

2. Ibid., 202.

3. Diana Meehan, *Ladies of the Evening: Women Characters of Prime-Time Television* (Metuchen, NJ: Scarecrow, 1983), 37.

4. Hesse-Biber and Carter, *Working Women in America*, 181.

5. Charles lives with the Pembroke family in the 1984–1985 seasons, and this changes to the Powell family in subsequent seasons.

Chapter 6

Conclusions

Analyzing televised housework identifies certain trends regarding gendered activities within the domestic sphere, the fluidity of familial roles, relationships between family members, and models of household management. By analyzing four decades of housework representations in television, regarding these domestic activities as maternal practice, this study reveals just over twenty significant trends.

1. Rather than marginalize the female, housework actively centers her, makes her visible, and underscores the importance of her work—the preservative love that is inherent to the work, and consequently, the strength that accompanies the commitment to recognize and meet the preservation demands others.
2. Housework functions as a form of communication and often competition for female characters (e.g., *Make Room for Daddy*, *The Goldbergs*, and later *Rhoda* and *Maude*).
3. Children recognize housework as love and approach females most often at these moments for emotional support. In this way, housework functions as an invitation.
4. In the 1950s, unsurprisingly, housewives are depicted as doing most of the household labor, but husbands assist wives with housework quite a bit in this decade. In fact, in comparison to the 1960s and 1970s, television depicts men as doing far more housework in the 1950s. These are usually the moments husbands and wives discuss important family matters.
5. In the 1960s, television depicts men performing far less housework than in the 1950s, and more shows include housekeepers or housekeeper-type characters (e.g., *My Three Sons*, *Hazel*, *The Brady Bunch*, *I Dream of Jeannie*, *Family Affair*, *The Munsters*, *The Jetsons*, and *Mayberry R.F.D.*).

6. When a show depicts a single male head of household, he either makes enough money to hire a housekeeper (e.g., *Family Affair, Diff'rent Strokes,* and *Benson*), or he has someone move in to function as a housekeeper (*My Three Sons, The Andy Griffith Show, I Dream of Jeannie,* and *Mayberry R.F.D.*), this usually occurs to benefit the housekeeper-character as much as the single male lead. When a show depicts a female head of household, she is depicted as not making enough money to hire help and is consequently responsible for her own housework. (*The Lucy Show* and *Here's Lucy* establish the trend in the 1960s, and it is furthered by *The Partridge Family, Rhoda, The Mary Tyler Moore Show, Laverne and Shirley,* and *Tabitha* in the 1970s.)

7. In the 1960s, television depicts women as "needing to be needed" through housework. (*The Andy Griffith Show, Mayberry R.F.D.,* and *I Dream of Jeannie* begin the trend in the 1960s, and it is furthered by *All in the Family, The Jeffersons,* and *Mary Hartman, Mary Hartman* in the 1970s.)

8. In opposition to the few housekeepers of the 1950s, the 1960s depicts housekeepers as being integrated into the family, performing housework in addition to emotional support for the family. Even though the housekeeper serves the family as a family member, the housekeeper's needs and desires are rarely addressed. (*Hazel, The Brady Bunch, Family Affair, The Jetsons,* and *The Munsters* establish this trend in the 1960s, and it is furthered in the 1970s by *Diff'rent Strokes, The Jeffersons,* and *Benson.*)

9. When a show depicts a single female as the head of household, her children are portrayed as sharing the household duties. (*The Lucy Show* and *Here's Lucy* establish the trend in the 1960s, and it is furthered in the 1970s by *The Partridge Family* and *The Facts of Life.*) When a show depicts a single male head of household, the children do not actively participate in the housework, as these tasks are left to the housekeeper-character (e.g., *The Andy Griffith Show, Family Affair, Mayberry R.F.D.* in the 1960s, and *Diff'rent Strokes* and *Benson* in the 1970s). The only exception to this rule occurs in the 1980s when the children are all female, as in *Gimme a Break!* In this case, the children share the housework, even with a housekeeper. Obviously, this underscores the gendered nature of televised housework.

10. When women are depicted as transitioning from being single to married within a series, they are depicted as doing much more housework once they are married (e.g., *I Dream of Jeannie* in the 1960s and *Rhoda* in the 1970s). When viewed as maternal practice, this is interpreted positively, as television portrays transitioning from self-service to serving others as being ultimately satisfying.

11. Television almost completely stops depicting men performing housework in the 1970s. Even when males are employed as housekeepers, their housework becomes nearly invisible in the 1970s (e.g., *Benson*).

12. When families employ housekeepers, they become the voice of reason for the family, always offering the proper advice. When the housekeeper is female, this advice addresses only the private, personal, domestic realm—the female realm (e.g., *The Brady Bunch*, *Hazel*, *Diff'rent Strokes*, and *Gimme a Break!*). When the housekeeper is male, television allows him to advise also in the public, professional realm—the male realm (e.g., *Benson*, *Who's the Boss*, and *Mr. Belvedere*).

13. In the 1970s, housework is depicted as therapy for women, furthering the notion that it is a natural female attribute (e.g., *All in the Family*, *Rhoda*, and *Mary Hartman, Mary Hartman*).

14. Television in the 1980s responds to the egregious lack of male household labor in the 1970s by creating a multitude of shows with male housekeepers (e.g., *Benson*, *Who's the Boss*, *Charles in Charge*, and *Mr. Belvedere*).

15. The 1980s is the first decade to depict unequivocally the female who is equally fulfilled by both a career and by homemaking (e.g., *Webster*, *The Cosby Show*, *Growing Pains*, and *Family Ties*).

16. The 1980s is also the first decade to depict women as making enough money to hire housekeepers. However, in this model, the housekeeper is hyper-masculinized and the sexual interactions between the professional woman and the male housekeeper are emphasized (e.g., *Who's the Boss*). When the professional male hires the female housekeeper, sexual attraction is not depicted as an issue (e.g., *Diff'rent Strokes* and *Gimme a Break!*).

17. The 1980s brings to the fore the issue of women performing double duty, working full-time, while still performing most of the household labor (e.g., *Growing Pains*, *Webster*, and *Roseanne*).

18. In the 1980s, television depicts egalitarian household management models as being most satisfying to females (e.g., *The Cosby Show*, *Charles in Charge*, and *Family Ties*).

19. Television in the 1980s reveals that fulfillment through serving others—through housework—can occur only when the others visibly benefit from that work. When those being served do not appear to benefit, television depicts housework as drudgery (e.g., *Mama's Family*).

20. Whereas the 1960s and 1970s depict housekeepers as family members who serve the family, with no attention paid to their own needs or desires, the 1980s depicts housekeepers who are more self-centered (e.g., *Gimme a Break!*, *Who's the Boss*, and *Charles in Charge*). This self-centeredness is not depicted negatively. In fact, the relationships between these 1980s

housekeepers and their families are depicted as being more equitable and reciprocal than the one-sided models of the 1960s and 1970s.

21. Television in the 1980s calls attention to the self-reflexive qualities of television through program intros that use images of family photographs or videos (e.g., *Webster, Growing Pains, Mr. Belvedere, Alf, My Two Dads, The Cosby Show,* and *Family Ties*). This also connects the past to the present, and more specifically, it connects past families and their household management models to present families and their household management models.

This analysis ends with the 1980s because models of household management become much more diffuse after this decade. Even in the 1980s, it becomes more difficult to identify trends, but still, some persist. After the 1980s, likely because of the popularity of cable and later streaming, patterns are less prevalent than in previous decades. It seems relevant, though, that so many popular television shows in the 1980s include program intros that incorporate the iconography of family photographs and videos, as this points specifically to one of the most significant contributions of this study. As Spigel claims, "television serves as one of our culture's primary sources for historical consciousness."[1] These 1980s introductions seem to reflect an acknowledgment that in order to appreciate the past, we must find ways to connect it to the present—an idea that goes beyond these program introductions, though, and informs the entirety of this analysis.

When I initially developed an interest in televised housework, it was because of the disconnect and similarities I found in television and my own reality. As an adolescent, I watched 1950s, 1960s, and 1970s television reruns with my mother, while she cheerfully folded laundry. Although it seemed appropriate at the time, I am struck now that I never offered to help her, and I believe this had something to do with the fact that the image of mom sitting on the couch in front of me, folding clothes, matched up with the image on the television screen—women performing housework exclusively in the 1970s. Yet, when I became a wife and mother myself, I didn't understand or subscribe to the notion that housework would be my job because I am a woman, even though I had spent a lifetime believing it was my mother's job simply because she was a woman. This study is the result of wanting to understand the extent to which television influenced my belief throughout life that housework was mom's job as an adult woman in the 1970s but not mine as an adult woman in 2014. In other words, to what extent did I not help mom because I didn't witness many televised children or men performing domestic labor in the 1950s, 1960s, 1970s, and 1980s?

This raises another point regarding how we perceive history based on the televised image, a point Spigel discusses, saying, "Television engages a kind of historical consciousness that remembers the past in order to believe in the progress of the present"[2]—something I recognized in the self-reflexive, family-photograph-montage introductions of 1980s television shows. Of course, one of my first misconceptions concerning the disconnect between my mother's function within my adolescent household model and my function in my own household later in life involved the idea that feminism had relieved me of these duties—that I was exercising an equality in my household that my mother could not necessarily exercise in hers. So much of what I considered to be mom's history involved what I had seen depicted in television, and since my present didn't match up with television's depiction of the past, I jumped to the elementary conclusion that times have changed—that we've come so far—and whereas a woman used to be responsible exclusively for her household management, we have progressed past that inequality in the present. (Honestly, I foolishly believed I inhabited a strength required in implementing an egalitarian approach to household management that perhaps my mother had not possessed.) In other words, I couldn't seem to think about the past without comparing it to the present, and considering I was born in the 1970s, much of my idea of the "past" in the 1950s, 1960s, and 1970s comes from what I had seen on television.

Spigel performed an experiment related to this with her college students in the 1990s, and her conclusions are relevant to my points here. She asked them to write down what they thought women were like in the 1950s, and most of their answers involved comparisons to women today, much like my assessments of my mother involve comparisons to my own roles. Spigel says the following:

> First, although I did not ask the women to compare the 1950s to the 1990s, their primary mode for thinking about the past was through comparison with the present—a situation that suggests that the past was relevant to the students insofar as it was pertinent to their own lives. In making the past relevant, they also engaged in a process of familiarization; they made sense of the past by describing it in terms of a repertoire of images with which they were acquainted. . . . the women used television as their key source of familiarization.[3]

I found that my own need to understand my role as a wife and mother, as a woman, was based on the disconnect I felt in comparing myself to memories of my mother's role in the 1970s and to the televised image. So this study evolved out of the same comparisons Spigel describes with her students, and my only way of rationalizing the differences was, in part, to blame television for my skewed sense of history, for planting stereotypes in my memory, for signifying mom's "job" in the 1970s as being exclusively responsible for the housework.

This study, however, has shown me that I could not be more wrong about these assumptions and conclusions. If we make things mean, as Hall states, then my twenty-first-century readings of televised housework from the 1950s, 1960s, 1970s, and 1980s likely differ greatly from the meanings made by the women of these eras. This is an obvious point, and thoughtlessly, I believed I could circumvent the fruitless activity of making assumptions regarding real mid-century interpretations by comparing the televised images to my own mother and to myself. It did not help that the research happened to reveal that 1970s television depicted less male domestic labor than any other decade—an image that was completely consistent with my own 1970s household as a child. But whereas I was wrong in my approach, by comparing mid-century televised images to my own mother, I recognized a greater point regarding housework and representations of housework. After finishing my research, I mentioned to my mother in passing what I had found, saying, "It's no wonder you were made to feel solely responsible for the household management in the 1970s; that's all we were seeing in television, too." Much to my surprise, my mother revealed that she had not been made to feel solely responsible for the housework and child-rearing. She *wanted* to do it, claiming she didn't always enjoy the tasks specifically—cleaning toilets, folding laundry, attending endless PTA meetings (i.e., the drudgery)—but she found total fulfillment in seeing us benefit from her work. And that's when it hit me that I had been stripping these televised women of similar qualities—of the strength that is inherent in my mother's statement. I had been guilty of erroneously viewing television women—and since television was my version of history, women in reality too—of the 1950s, 1960s, and 1970s as "passive dupes of patriarchy."[4] I had been guilty of, as Spigel states, celebrating "women's enlightenment in the present at the expense of undercutting their agency in the past."[5]

My mother is not every woman, and televised women do not reflect every reality, but my mother's statement regarding housework is a commonality I found to be consistent in televised housework from every decade. I viewed the fulfillment she claimed in television of every decade. I witnessed it not just in housewives, and not just in working women. I viewed it in any televised characters who experienced others benefitting from their life-preserving domestic labors. This fulfillment found through recognizing and meeting the demands of others reflects strength, and that realization inspired this study and informed my conclusions. There exists in women, both in reality and representation, an unparalleled strength that is inherent in these domestic activities of maternal practice—activities that exist almost exclusively for the benefit of others. This is the same reason my favorite memories of mom involve her performing many of these tasks. Her housework communicated ultimate love to me, and now it also communicates strength. It is *that* strength that televised housework, and hopefully this analysis, ultimately brings to the fore.

NOTES

1. Spigel, *Dreamhouse,* 368.
2. Ibid., 362.
3. Ibid., 367–368.
4. Elaine Tyler May, *Homeward Bound: American Families in the Cold War Era* (New York: Basic Books, 1988). Quoted in Spigel's *Welcome to the Dreamhouse* on page 362.
5. Spigel, *Dreamhouse,* 362.

Bibliography

Barthes, Roland. *Image-Music-Text*. New York: Hill and Wang, 1977.

Bassin, Donna, Margaret Honey, and Meryle Mahrer Kaplan, eds. *Representations of Motherhood*. New Haven: Yale UP, 1994.

Douglas, Susan J. *Where the Girls Are: Growing Up Female with the Mass Media*. New York: Three Rivers Press, 1995.

Douglas, Susan J., and Meredith W. Michaels. *The Mommy Myth: The Idealization of Motherhood and How It Has Undermined Women*. New York: Free Press, 2004.

Earle, David M. *All Man!: Hemingway, 1950s Men's Magazines, and the Masculine Persona*. Kent, Ohio: The Kent State UP, 2009.

Elshtain, Jean Bethke. *Public Man, Private Woman*. Princeton: Princeton UP, 1981.

Feasey, Rebecca. *From Happy Homemaker to Desperate Housewives: Motherhood and Popular Television*. London: Anthem Press, 2012.

Federici, Silvia. *Revolution at Point Zero: Housework, Reproduction, and Feminist Struggle*. Oakland, CA: PM Press, 2012.

Fiske, John. *Television Culture*. New York: Routledge, 2011.

Friedan, Betty. *The Feminine Mystique* (1963). Tenth Anniversary Edition. New York: W.W. Norton & Company, Inc., 1974.

———. "Television and the Feminine Mystique." *TV Guide: The First 25 Years*, J.S. Harris, ed. (New York: New American Library, 1980): 93–98.

Hall, Stuart, ed. *Representation: Cultural Representations and Signifying Practices*. London: Sage, 1997.

Haralovich, Mary Beth. "Sitcoms and Suburbs: Positioning the 1950s Homemaker." *Quarterly Review of Film and Video* 11, no. 1 (May 1989): 61–83.

Hesse-Biber, Sharlene, and Gregg Lee Carter. *Working Women in America: Split Dreams*. New York: Oxford UP, 2000.

Humphreys, Kristi. "Supernatural Housework." *Home Sweat Home*. Elizabeth Patton and Mimi Choi, eds. Lanham, MD: Rowman and Littlefield, 2014.

Kaplan, E. Ann. *Motherhood and Representation*. New York: Routledge, 1992.

Kanner, Bernice. "From *Father Knows Best* to *The Simpsons*—On TV, Parenting Has Lost Its Halo," in Sylvia Ann Hewlett, Nancy Rankin, and Cornel West (Eds.) *Taking Parenting Public: The Case for a New Social Movement*. Lanham: Rowman & Littlefield, 2002.

Karlyn, Kathleen Rowe. *Unruly Girls, Unrepentant Mothers: Redefining Feminism on Screen*. Austin: U of Texas P, 2011.

Kutulas, Judy. "Who Rules the Roost?: Sitcom Family Dynamics from the Cleavers to the Osbournes," in Mary M. Dalton and Laura R. Linder (Eds.) *The Sitcom Reader: America Viewed and Skewed*. Albany: State U of New York P, 2005.

Leibman, Nina C. *Living Room Lectures: The Fifties Family in Film and Television*. Austin, TX: University of Texas Press, 1995.

Marc, David. *Comic Visions: Television Comedy and American Culture*. Boston: Unwin Hyman, 1989.

Maasik, Sonia, and Jack Solomon. *Signs of Life in the U.S.A.: Readings on Popular Culture for Writers*. Boston: Bedford/St. Martin's, 2012.

May, Elaine Tyler. *Homeward Bound: American Families in the Cold War Era*. New York: Basic Books, 1988.

McRobbie, Angela. *The Aftermath of Feminism: Gender, Culture and Social Change*. Los Angeles: Sage, 2009.

Meehan, Diana. *Ladies of the Evening: Women Characters of Prime-Time Television*. Metuchen, NJ: Scarecrow, 1983.

Neuhaus, Jessamyn. *Married to the Mop: Housework and Housewives in Modern American Advertising*. New York: Palgrave Macmillan, 2011.

Rich, Adrienne (1976). *Of Woman Born: Motherhood as Experience and Institution*. New York: W. W. Norton & Company, 1995.

Ruddick, Sara. *Maternal Thinking: Toward a Politics of Peace*. Boston: Beacon Press, 1989.

Spigel, Lynn. *Make Room for TV: Television and the Family Ideal in Postwar America*. Chicago: U of Chicago P, 1992.

———. *Welcome to the Dream House: Popular Media and Postwar Suburbs*. Durham, NC: Duke University Press, 2011.

Stacey, Judith. "The New Conservative Feminism." *Feminist Studies*. Vol. 9, no. 3 (Autumn, 1983), 559–583.

VIDEOGRAPHY

(I screened the episodes from season one of each series.)
The Goldbergs (1949–1956)
I Love Lucy (1951–1957)
My Little Margie (1952–1955)
The Best of The Adventures of Ozzie and Harriet (1952–1966)
Make Room for Daddy (1953–1964)
Father Knows Best (1954–1960)
The Honeymooners (1955–1956)

The Real McCoys (1957–1963)
Leave It to Beaver (1957–1963)
The Donna Reed Show (1958–1966)
Dennis the Menace (1959–1963)
My Three Sons (1960–1972)
The Andy Griffith Show (1960–1968)
Hazel (1961–1966)
The Dick Van Dyke Show (1961–1966)
The Beverly Hillbillies (1962–1971)
The Lucy Show (1962–1968)
The Jetsons (1962–1963)
The Patty Duke Show (1963–1966)
Petticoat Junction (1963–1970)
Gilligan's Island (1964–1967)
Bewitched (1964–1972)
The Munsters (1964–1966)
The Addams Family (1964–1966)
Green Acres (1965–1971)
I Dream of Jeannie (1965–1970)
Family Affair (1966–1971)
Here's Lucy (1968–1974)
Mayberry R.F.D. (1968–1971)
The Brady Bunch (1969–1974)
The Partridge Family (1970–1974)
The Mary Tyler Moore Show (1970–1977)
All in the Family (1971–1979)
Maude (1972–1978)
Good Times (1974–1979)
Happy Days (1974–1984)
Rhoda (1974–1978)
The Jeffersons (1975–1985)
Laverne and Shirley (1976–1983)
Tabitha (1976–1978)
Soap (1977–1981)
Three's Company (1977–1984)
Diff'rent Strokes (1978–1986)
Benson (1979–1986)
The Facts of Life (1979–1988)
Gimme a Break! (1981–1987)
Family Ties (1982–1989)
Silver Spoons (1982–1987)
Webster (1983–1989)
The Cosby Show (1984–1992)
Who's the Boss (1984–1992)
Charles In Charge (1984–1990)

Growing Pains (1985–1992)
Mr. Belvedere (1985–1990)
Golden Girls (1985–1992)
Mama's Family (1986–1990)
Alf (1986–1990)
My Two Dads (1987–1990)
Roseanne (1988–1997)
Family Matters (1989–1998)

Index

About the Author

Kristi Rowan Humphreys is Assistant Professor of Critical Studies and Artistic Practice and Coordinator of the Fine Arts Doctoral Program in Art at Texas Tech University in Lubbock. Having completed an interdisciplinary Ph.D. in the Humanities, Aesthetic Studies at The University of Texas at Dallas, she specializes in gender media and popular culture studies, film musicals and musical theater, and the visual culture of novelist William Faulkner. Recent publications explore pop culture representations of housework and domesticity, motherhood and fatherhood, and magic and religion. Also a working stage and commercial actress, she is a member of Actors' Equity Association, and a recipient of a Kennedy Center American College Theatre Festival award for performance.

Most important, she is a proud wife to Chris and mom to Rowan and Lawson. She hails from the small town of Lorena, Texas, where she was reared to love God, family, and the Baylor Bears.